STOP SEARCHING *for* YOUR CHILD'S CALLING

STOP SEARCHING *for* YOUR CHILD'S CALLING

A FRAMEWORK FOR DIRECTING THEIR CAREER PATH

C.W. LEE

CORAL TREE PRESS

Note on Authorship & AI Tools: The frameworks, theology, and core arguments in this book are the original work of the author. AI tools were used to draft prose and case studies based on the author's ideas and direction. All content was edited by the author. The author accepts full responsibility for the final text, its logic, and its accuracy.

Credits: Book designed by Mark Karis

Published by Coral Tree Press

First Edition: April 2026

ISBN: 979-8-234-04364-1

Printed in the United States of America

stopsearchingseries.com | contact@stopsearchingseries.com

CONTENTS

Preface i

PART I: THE FRAMEWORK

1 The Modern Gray Zone 3

2 Gift-Love 11

3 The Knowledge Problem 19

4 The Foundation 27

5 The 1+3 Framework 39

6 Implementation 57

7 Formation Begins Young 69

8 Formation and Daughters 79

9 The Child's Posture 87

10 Conclusion 97

Appendix A: Framework Diagram 103
Appendix B: Logic Chain 104
Appendix C: Glossary of Key Terms 107
References 110

PART II: CASE STUDIES

Introduction 115
CASE #1: Sam—High Durable Agency vs. Passion Path 117
CASE #2: Emma—The Cost of Deferral 127
CASE #3: Claire—Success but Destroyed Relationship 139
CASE #4: David—Agency Without Faith 147
CASE #5: Ethan—Missions vs. Durable Agency 155

PREFACE

I wrote this book because I watched good parents, acting from genuine love, produce outcomes they never intended—some who directed past the point where direction was building anything, others who deferred to children's preferences until those children drifted into their thirties without the capacity for independent household formation. And I watched good children rebel against legitimate direction, conflating productive struggle with oppression, straining relationships that might never fully recover. These failure modes produced adults who struggled and families who didn't understand what had gone wrong.

I am a practicing physician currently raising four young children and applying these principles in real time. I do not write from the safety of hindsight but from the uncertainty of active formation. I may be wrong about application in ways I cannot yet see. What I am confident about is the framework's structure: that durable agency is a more concrete criterion than calling, that gift-love can be distinguished from need-love, that productive struggle differs from systemic breakdown, and that parental authority has a proper endpoint.

I expect disagreement—indeed, I am publishing this work precisely to invite it. Christians of good faith applying this framework will reach different conclusions about the same child in the same circumstances. One parent will read these principles and conclude that engineering is required; another will conclude that literature, pursued with discipline, satisfies the Expansion Principle for their particular child. The framework does not eliminate such disagreement. It structures disagreement around the right questions: Does this build durable agency? Am I acting from gift-love? Am I watching for breakdown? Am I preparing them for a life of service to God?

My background shapes my examples, which lean toward demanding professional training. This reflects my own formation, not a claim that such paths are uniquely valuable. Readers in different circumstances will need to adapt the principles to paths I cannot illustrate. Parents directing their son toward a master electrician apprenticeship are applying the framework as faithfully as parents directing their daughter toward dental school—the framework's criteria remain the same, but the paths differ based on family situation, resources, and the particular child. Directing formation does not mean overriding a child's every decision—it means that the parent, not the child, determines how much freedom is appropriate and when.

Some readers will arrive skeptical—their own children turned out fine without active direction, or they themselves succeeded without it. I address why such cases do not invalidate the framework in Chapter 1.

This framework is a web, not a list. Its insights—about calling, about parental motive, about the child's posture, about when authority ends, among others—depend on each other. Readers who extract one without the others will likely misapply it.

A framework that grants parents real authority can be misused by parents acting in bad faith. This book is written for Christian parents acting in good faith who want to get formation right—not for parents weaponizing authority. If you are reading this book to justify formation that your child, counselors, or church leaders have told you is harmful, the Accountability Constraint applies to you. This framework does not exist to validate decisions you have already made; it exists to structure decisions you have not yet made—or to prompt reconsideration of decisions that aren't working.

The stakes are high. Children who drift into adulthood without durable agency face structural barriers to faithful service that their parents could have prevented. Children who break under formation that should have been adjusted carry lifelong wounds. Children whose parents cannot release authority become adults who cannot fully become adults. These outcomes matter eternally, not just economically.

I am not a theologian. I needed a framework and couldn't find one. I offer this framework not as the final word but as a contribution to a conversation that the church needs to have more rigorously—an operational vocabulary for thinking about formation, not a comprehensive theology of vocation. This book's core principles apply broadly, though it is written from within the conservative evangelical tradition. Test it. Challenge it. The formation of the next generation is too important to be left to intuition, cultural defaults, or the unexamined assumption that whatever worked for us will work for them.

PART I

THE FRAMEWORK

1

THE MODERN GRAY ZONE

By the time you know whether your parenting worked or not, it will be too late to fix it.

He is twenty-seven. He graduated college, works in marketing, and makes a decent living. He is not in crisis. He calls on birthdays and comes home for Christmas. This is the family nobody worries about. The parents had a philosophy—give him space, let him find his way.

When the company downsizes, he'll be competing against younger candidates with sharper skills—and he won't have the margin to absorb the hit. When his marriage hits a rough patch he won't have the relational depth to fight for it. When his faith is tested, he won't have the community to hold him up. His parents loved him. They also let him set his own course at sixteen because it felt like respect. The absence of visible failure became their measure of success. But the absence of crisis is not the same as the presence of capacity. "Fine at twenty-seven" does not mean "prepared for forty."

And then there is the family that looks like a success story. Their daughter is a surgeon. She graduated top of her class and earns more than her parents ever did. She goes to church. She visits for holidays. Her marriage is stable. Her parents are proud—and from where they sit, the strategy worked.

But her faith is routine, not conviction. Her visits home are dutiful, not deep. Her marriage functions because both spouses avoid conflict rather than resolve it. Her parents do not see this, because everything they taught her to value is firmly in place. When eighty-hour work weeks grind against a marriage built on avoidance rather than trust, it won't bend—it will break. When an injury ends her career, she won't have an identity apart from the one her parents built for her.

In both families, the parents believe that formation went well. In both, the evidence suggests otherwise—but only if you know what to look for.

"Fine" may not be as good as it looks in either family. The marketing son makes decent decisions—but he has never been forced to make hard ones under real pressure. He does not know what sharper judgment feels like, because adequate results feel like good results when no one has ever required more of him. The surgeon has professional excellence—but her parents never taught her that faith and relationships matter as much as achievement. Neither family knows what they are missing. The parents who never pushed through hard conversations with their child rarely have hard conversations from their child. The relationships are pleasant because they are shallow. People cannot miss what they never had. That is the trap of "fine." Everything feels adequate, so nothing feels urgent, so nothing changes.

Many parents can see themselves in one of these two families. But there are two more.

He is thirty-two, living in a studio apartment, on his fourth career pivot since college. He is not lazy. He is not foolish. He is undirected—and his parents, good people who loved him, don't know what they could have done differently. They offered options, encouraged exploration, and trusted him to find his own way. It felt like respect. It felt like love. It was also a choice—a formation decision with consequences they didn't foresee.

Meanwhile, other parents face the opposite fear. Their son is twenty-four and at a top dental school. His parents chose the field and he resents them for it. They do not have a close relationship with their son, and they wonder if it was worth it.

Four families. Not one produced what the parents actually wanted: an adult child with the sustained capacity to weather adversity, maintain deep relationships, and serve God faithfully—not just at twenty-five, but at forty and beyond. Some readers will not see their family in any of these four. Neither did these parents.

Beneath all these outcomes lies a question: How should parents direct their child's formation—and when should they stop? This book offers a principle along with three constraints to help parents answer that question.

THE CRISIS OF THE MODERN GRAY ZONE

This framework addresses a distinctly modern problem. For most of human history, children inherited their parents' trade, married young, and established households by their early twenties—all under the watchful eye of a community that provided natural accountability. Today, three shifts have created an unprecedented "gray zone" of formation.

First, infinite choice has replaced inherited vocation. With so many career paths available, many parents have concluded that the best approach is to step back and let children find their own way. This isn't indecision—it's a deliberate philosophy. But it assumes that children can identify what builds long-term capacity better than parents can.

Second, modern success has become a feedback black hole. A child can appear successful on paper—prestigious university, accumulating credentials—while lacking in ways that don't show up on a resume: few deep friendships, shallow faith, underdeveloped character, strained family relationships.

Third, the period between ages eighteen and thirty has become unprecedented territory. Extended education and delayed marriage have left many adults unsettled—cycling through jobs, staying single with no clear path toward marriage, lacking purpose beyond immediate preferences, and building nothing that lasts.

WHY "IT WORKED FOR US" PROVES NOTHING

Some parents will read this and object: "We didn't direct our children, and they became an engineer or a successful entrepreneur. We must have done something right." Three errors corrupt this reasoning.

First, unrecognized formation. These parents often formed

their children without recognizing it. The child who "chose" basketball started playing because Dad played with him in the driveway. Over years, what began as relational connection became genuine interest. The parent says "he just naturally loved it," but that love was shaped by hundreds of hours of formation the parent provided without calling it formation—and by hundreds of hours not spent on soccer or swimming. In the same manner, a police officer will form a child just by the way he lives—its demands, its rewards, the opportunity it provides to serve others—long before anyone discusses career direction. By the time the parent says "follow your passion," eighteen years of proximity have already shaped what this child considers a realistic path. The parent credits the child's autonomy. The household was the formation. All parents form their children, both by decisions they make and the decisions they do not make. The difference is that some choose their direction consciously while others shape their children's paths without recognizing it—then attribute the outcome to the child's autonomous choice.

Second, survivorship bias. Parents whose children succeeded tell stories. Parents whose children drifted into their thirties without direction do not write books or offer advice at dinner parties. The approach that produced one family's successful engineer also produced another family's struggling thirty-four-year-old—but only the success stories get cited as evidence.

Third, parents cannot know whether their child succeeded *because of* their approach or *despite* it. A child with high native ability and favorable circumstances might turn out fine through many paths—including paths that would fail children without those advantages. One family's outcome proves nothing about what works reliably.

Formation must therefore be evaluated by a reliable strategy, not exceptional outcomes. The old maps fail here. "Just be strict" ignores modern complexity. "Just be their friend" increases the risk of drift. This framework offers a third way: formation logic designed for a high-choice world—where parental authority is real but bounded, and ultimately oriented toward launching children into independent, faithful adulthood.

WHY "FINE" IS NOT FORMED

Many parents will not see their child in any of these families. Their children hold steady jobs in areas they choose, pay their rent, and maintain cordial relationships. These parents have no crisis to solve. They arrived at this book by accident and they are already wondering whether it applies to them.

This framework argues that it does. "Fine" describes a current condition. It does not describe a capacity. The question is not whether a child can hold a moderate job in a stable economy. The question is whether that child has the sustained ability to act independently when life applies real pressure—a layoff at thirty-eight, a difficult marriage, a season of suffering that demands character no one required them to build.

Parents who measure success by the absence of crisis have adopted a standard that only reveals its weakness when crisis arrives. By then, it is too late to build what was never built—not because the parents failed to love, but because the parents confused peace with preparation.

The relationship tells the same story. "Not close, but not estranged" often results from years of avoiding the very conversations that build trust. The relationship stays comfortable because it stays shallow. That is not closeness. It is comfort mistaken for connection.

These parents were not operating without a framework. The parent who says "I am letting him find his own way" has adopted a framework—one that treats personal preference as a reliable guide and the absence of crisis as evidence of success. The parent who says "I am trusting God with her future" has adopted a framework—one that treats non-intervention as faith and passivity as spiritual maturity. The problem is not that these parents lacked a framework. Every parent has one. The problem is that an unexamined framework cannot be tested, corrected, or held accountable—and by the time its failures become visible, the window for formation has closed.

2

GIFT-LOVE

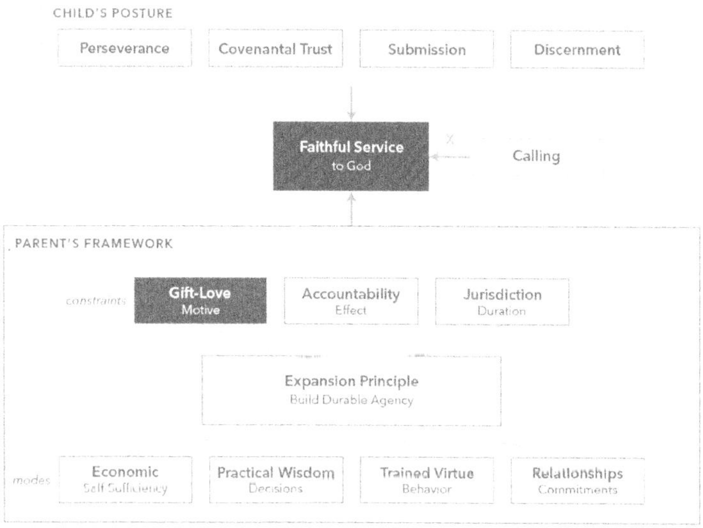

GIFT-LOVE

The first thing an examined framework requires is an honest assessment of motive. C. S. Lewis, in *The Four Loves*, distinguishes two forms of parental love: gift-love and need-love Gift-love is the desire to give, serve, and sacrifice for your child's good—with no strings attached. Need-love is different. It is the parent's longing to be needed, to feel secure, to have someone fill the emptiness inside them.

Here's the paradox. A parent who believes they're sacrificing purely for their child may be blind to how much they *need* to be needed. And this is the danger that Lewis saw so clearly: when gift-love gets tangled up with unacknowledged need-love, it turns into control and manipulation. It wounds the very child it claims to serve.

But what does "the child's good" actually mean? Many Christians assume that parents go wrong when they push a direction the child doesn't naturally want—when they override the child's inclinations or apparent calling. But as I'll argue in Chapter 3, a calling isn't something we can reliably know ahead of time. That means that parents need a different standard for judging whether their direction actually serves their child—and that standard is durable agency.

WHY GIFT-LOVE IS HARD

A daughter wants art school. Her parents are directing her toward optometry school because they believe that it builds more durable agency. They are acting from gift-love, genuinely trying to protect her from what they see as a foolish, shortsighted decision—she's eighteen, focused on present preference, blind to realities they understand from decades of adult life. But when she says, "You don't care what I want. You just want to control me," something shifts.

Formation decisions carry weight. Parents might feel anxious about whether they are making the right call. They might feel fear about the relationship. But often, what parents feel most is plain frustration—she won't listen, she can't see what's obvious. They're exhausted from having the same argument over and over again. These are normal responses to exercising authority under uncertainty. They don't automatically signify need-love. But they create the conditions where need-love can enter.

The question is what happens next. Does the frustration stay focused on the child and her good—on genuinely wanting her to flourish, even when she fights back? Or does it become about the parent? About needing to win the argument? About proving they're right? About what her resistance says about their competence? About refusing to ask "what if I'm wrong?" because the question feels like weakness. When does frustration cross the line? When does frustration about her stubbornness become need for her compliance? When does commitment to the path become inability to adjust—because backing down would feel like losing? That's when need-love has taken over.

Need-love does not just mean wanting good outcomes. Need-love means *needing* the child's outcomes to prove something about the parent—to show that the parent is okay, competent, or worthy. When formation is driven by that need, it corrupts practical decision: parents can't adjust when paths aren't working because the breakdown feels like their failure. They can't grant space for struggle because the child's struggle threatens their competence.

But need-love doesn't only corrupt directive parents. It corrupts permissive parents too—just differently. Some permissive parents defer to their child's preferences because they need their child's approval. They can't bear conflict. They need to be the understanding parent, the one who "gets it." That's need-love wearing softer clothes.

There's a subtler version still. Some parents genuinely believe that not directing is gift-love—that respecting their child's autonomy is the most loving thing they can do. This sounds like principle, and sometimes it is. But it can also be need-love in disguise. "I don't want to impose" may mask "I'm afraid they'll resent me." "I trust them to find their way" may mask "I don't want responsibility if it goes wrong." "It's their life" may mask "I can't tolerate the conflict that direction would require."

The test depends on where the temptation lies. For directive parents: Can they adjust when the path isn't working—without feeling like a failure? For permissive parents: Can they hold a boundary while their child is upset with them? Gift-love can do both. It can be the bad guy for a season and adjust when evidence demands it. Need-love—whether it controls or capitulates—can't.

So how do parents direct from gift-love when pulls toward need-love are real? Not by trying harder to be selfless. The foundation is the gospel.

THE GOSPEL GROUND

The Father calls His children "beloved"—not because of parenting success or a child's achievements, but because of Christ's finished work. A parent's standing before God was secured at the cross, not at their child's graduation.

This is what holds parents steady when formation gets hard. When a daughter accuses her parent of control, the parent doesn't need her to understand—their worth isn't on trial. When she resists, they can absorb it without defensiveness—they're not requiring her validation. When they wonder if they're making the right call, they can hold their direction with conviction or adjust if evidence accumulates—either way, Christ's grace covers them.

The gospel enables gift-love not by eliminating anxiety but

by giving secure ground beneath it. Identity is settled. Worth is established. The Father's approval doesn't fluctuate with children's outcomes. This security frees parents to direct from the child's good rather than their own need.

This gospel foundation also protects against another mistake: thinking that character can be built in a child through sheer effort. Yes, formation takes work—years of discipline, structure, and hard paths. But the change that happens in the child is grace. As Paul writes, "Work out your salvation with fear and trembling, for it is God who works in you, both to will and to work for his good pleasure" (Philippians 2:12–13). Parents do the work. God does the transformation. When parents direct a child toward a demanding path, they are not manufacturing virtue by willpower. They are giving God the raw material He typically uses to shape character.

THE SPIRIT'S WORK IN FORMATION

The Spirit's role in all of this should not be overlooked. When parents direct a child toward a demanding path, they are not relying on their own wisdom alone. The Spirit guides parents who pray, stay in Scripture, and stay connected to their church. And He works through ordinary means: discernment gets sharper through prayer, judgment gets shaped by the Word, blind spots get exposed by community. This doesn't mean that parents will never get it wrong—even Spirit-led parents make mistakes, which is why the Accountability Constraint matters. But it does mean that faithful formation is a spiritual discipline, not just a parenting strategy. Parents who neglect prayer, Scripture, and community while directing their child's path have cut themselves off from the main ways that God shapes the heart from which those decisions are made.

A parent grounded in these disciplines can respond to resistance from a place of security rather than defensiveness. When a daughter says "You don't care what I want," a parent can respond: "I hear your anger, and I understand this is hard. I'm directing you toward optometry school because I genuinely believe it will expand your capacity for faithful service. I might be wrong, but I'm acting from what I believe serves your good, and I'm watching carefully to adjust if this path causes breakdown rather than growth."

Where does that security come from? Not from believing that the choice is perfect, but from believing Christ already made the parent acceptable to God. Formation from gift-love isn't about being a perfect parent—it's about being a redeemed parent, slowly learning to parent from the security of being perfectly loved.

DESIRES REORDERED

The gospel does not only secure a parent's identity. It reorders what parents want.

Formation decisions flow from desire. A parent whose deepest desire is worldly success will form differently than a parent whose deepest desire is faithfulness to God—even if both direct toward the same demanding path. The heart behind the decision shapes everything: how a parent responds to resistance, whether a parent can adjust when things go wrong, and whether the child experiences gift-love or need-love in the process.

The problem is that desire drifts. Parents who began from gift-love can find their desires slowly reordering around achievement, control, or status without noticing the shift. A mother who started by wanting her daughter to develop resilience may gradually desire to see her daughter outperform her peers. A father who started by wanting his son to build capacity may gradually begin needing his son's success to validate his own parenting. The shift is subtle. It happens in degrees. And the parent experiencing it is usually the last person to see it.

The gospel is the corrective—not as a one-time event but as a daily recalibration. When parents are regularly reminded of what Christ has done, their desires realign: what God wants for this child becomes more important than what I want for this child. What that recalibration looks like will differ from moment to moment. At times, it is Scripture. At other times, it is prayer, or remembering what God has done in the parent's own life, or honest fellowship, or worship that draws the heart back to Christ in the middle of a hard week. The means vary. What matters is that the gospel stays close enough to correct the drift before it corrupts the decision.

Parents who apply this framework without regularly returning to the gospel will find their desires drifting toward the very need-love the framework is designed to prevent. The framework provides structure. The gospel provides the heart from which that structure is rightly used.

3

THE KNOWLEDGE PROBLEM

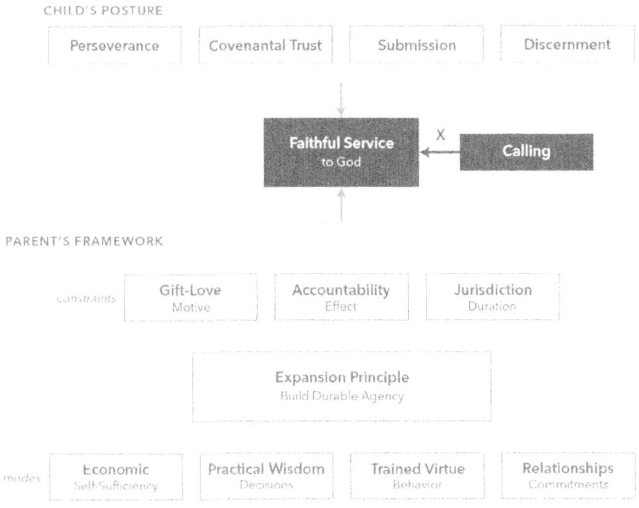

This raises an immediate question: If parents have authority to direct formation, what guides their decisions? Answering this requires understanding what can and cannot be known about the child's calling—God's ultimate purpose for them in this life.

Many Christian writings on vocation emphasize introspection and self-discovery—find your passion, listen for God's voice, discover your calling. Some look to observable aptitudes and interests as indicators of divine purpose, assuming that a child gifted in music is "meant" for music, or that a child who struggles with biology is "not called" to medicine. But these approaches assume that calling can ordinarily be known—through Scripture, circumstance, prayer, inner peace, or community counsel. That assumption deserves testing.

Consider a man—call him John—facing two job opportunities. One is out of state: higher pay, work he is passionate about, a chance to serve a specific community in ways that feel deeply meaningful. The other is in his hometown: lower pay, aspects of the role he dislikes, but proximity to parents and siblings who matter to him. Both are legitimate. Neither is sinful.

The standard tools for figuring out calling all apply—and none of them resolve the question.

Scripture? John searches for biblical guidance. He finds verses affirming the use of gifts for God's glory, which supports the out-of-state role. He also finds verses commanding faithfulness to family and honoring parents, which supports staying home. Scripture gives him principles that apply to both options, but it does not tell him which job to take. The Bible speaks clearly on matters of sin and obedience. It does not typically provide vocational specificity between two legitimate paths.

Circumstance? God opened both doors. One could argue that God opened the door out of state because He wants John doing work that matches his gifts in a community that needs him. One could equally argue that God opened the opportunity at home so that John could be near family—because presence with the people God gave him matters more than career success. The same set of circumstances supports opposite conclusions.

Prayer? John prays earnestly. Unless God speaks directly—and for most Christians in most decisions, He does not—prayer produces sincerity without certainty. The posture is right, but John emerges from prayer still holding the same question.

Inner peace? John feels more peace about the out-of-state role. But peace often reflects comfort and desire, not divine direction. A person can feel deep peace about a decision simply because it aligns with what they already wanted. Peace can also reflect avoidance—the hometown role involves work John dislikes, and the discomfort he feels may be resistance to difficulty rather than the Spirit's warning. Peace cannot distinguish between "God is confirming this" and "I prefer this."

Community affirmation? John asks his church, his friends, his mentors. But John chose his church and his friends—and in general, people connect with those who share their values and assumptions. A friend with distant family relationships may not see the value of proximity. A friend who has made significant sacrifices for family may advocate for staying without fully understanding how important the work is to John. If John's community leans toward ambition, they will affirm ambition. If they lean toward family, they will affirm staying. Even seeking *diverse* counsel — voices that might challenge him — does not solve the problem. The question itself has no answer accessible to any human observer. Diverse counsel produces diverse answers, and John must still decide which counsel to weight more heavily.

Some will object that this analysis leaves out the Holy Spirit—that the Spirit guides believers into truth and illuminates decisions that human reasoning alone cannot resolve. This objection is serious, as the Spirit's work in John's life is real and essential. But consider what the Spirit actually does in a decision like this. The Spirit convicts John of selfish motives. The Spirit produces in John a genuine desire to glorify God rather than serve himself. The Spirit shapes John into the kind of man who will serve faithfully wherever he lands. This is the Spirit's sanctifying work—it determines *why* John chooses, which is the most important question. But sanctified motivation does not dictate *which* option to choose. A man who genuinely wants to glorify God can glorify God in either city. The Spirit ensures that John's heart is oriented rightly. The Spirit does not typically function as a compass pointing to one city over the other.

Now suppose all five indicators—Scripture, circumstances, prayer, peace, and community—point in the same direction. How does John know whether this convergence reflects genuine divine guidance or one bias building on itself? If all five indicators lean the same way, their agreement proves consistency, not truth. Five instruments calibrated to the same bias will produce the same reading, but the reading may still not reveal calling.

This is not a failure of John's faith. It is a structural limitation of the tools available to all of us. And if an adult with full spiritual maturity and access to every standard indicator still cannot determine with certainty which path represents God's calling—the implications for formation are significant. The claim that parents can discern a child's calling at sixteen, or that a child's self-reported sense of calling should override parental direction, rests on an even weaker foundation.

External signs offer no more certainty: A child who struggles with biology might simply need to develop perseverance—not change to a different path. A child's visible talents show what they can do, not necessarily what God has called them to do. Those talents reflect the few activities the child has actually tried—and what the child has tried was shaped by the parents' choices. The child who 'naturally' excels in music may not have attempted robotics, baseball, or culinary arts—and might be better at any of them. But no one will ever know, because the child has only been exposed to a tiny slice of what exists. Parents who treat their child's current strengths as proof of God's design are drawing conclusions from a small sample. God's sovereignty is real—but it extends to the parents He gave the child, not only to the experiences that shaped the child's interests. One cannot claim providence for the experiences that confirm a child's preferences and deny it for the authority that redirects them.

THE BIBLICAL PATTERN

Scripture confirms this pattern—and goes further. "The heart is more deceitful than all else and is desperately sick" (Jeremiah 17:9). Children's claims about their calling cannot be fully trusted—they may genuinely believe that they know what God wants for them and still be wrong.

Apart from rare direct revelation, God typically forms His servants through extended processes of obedience, responsibility, and constraint, with calling becoming visible only in hindsight.

Consider Joseph. Sold into slavery by his brothers at seventeen (Genesis 37:28), he spent years as a servant in Potiphar's house, where he learned Egyptian language, customs, and household administration (Genesis 39:1–6). Falsely accused, he was imprisoned for years more, where he managed the prison and interpreted dreams for fellow prisoners (Genesis 39:20–23, 40:1–23). None of this pointed toward his eventual role. Joseph had no prophecy telling him he would govern Egypt. His father Jacob had no revelation that the son he mourned as dead would save the family from famine. The capacities that Joseph built—administrative skill, wisdom under pressure, patience through injustice, fluency in Egyptian culture—served purposes that no one could have anticipated during the long years of suffering. When Joseph finally told his brothers, "As for you, you meant evil against me, but God meant it for good in order to bring about this present result, to preserve many people alive" (Genesis 50:20), he was making sense of a calling that became visible only in retrospect.

Paul's formation followed a different pattern—directed training toward an anticipated purpose that God redirected entirely. Born a Roman citizen in Tarsus (Acts 22:3), Paul was sent to Jerusalem to study under Gamaliel, one of the most respected rabbis of his generation. His parents presumably directed him toward this rigorous education expecting he would become a leader in Jewish religious life. The training was exceptional: Paul describes himself as "a Hebrew of Hebrews; as to the law, a Pharisee … as to righteousness under the law, blameless" (Philippians 3:5–6). He mastered Torah, learned sophisticated argumentation, and absorbed the interpretive traditions of Pharisaic Judaism. Yet God used this formation for entirely different purposes than anyone intended. The same training that made Paul a zealous persecutor of Christians (Acts 8:3, 9:1–2) later equipped him to argue persuasively in synagogues (Acts 17:2–3), engage Greek philosophers on their own terms (Acts 17:22–31), and write theologically sophisticated letters that would shape Christian doctrine for millennia. Paul's parents directed his formation well. They simply had no way of knowing what it was for.

This pattern repeats throughout Scripture. Moses, Esther, Daniel, Nehemiah—in each case, God's purposes became visible only after formation had done its work. These are exceptional figures—but that strengthens the point. If calling was unknowable even for those God had extraordinary purposes for, ordinary parents have even less reason to expect advance clarity. Parents who wait for advance clarity about their child's calling wait for something that Scripture does not promise.

Developmental psychology points to the same conclusion. Identity isn't discovered pre-formed—it's built through sustained commitment.[2] College students change majors frequently—about thirty percent switch at least once within three years, with some estimates much higher.[3] This aligns with what philosopher Alasdair MacIntyre observed: the internal sense of purpose people describe as a 'calling' typically emerges after submitting to the demands of a discipline, not before.[4] The eighteen-year-old who resists a plumbing apprenticeship may become the twenty-five-year-old master plumber earning six figures who can't imagine doing anything else—not because the trade was always their calling, but because formation created competence and competence created meaning.

FAILURE DOESN'T REVEAL CALLING

This is the less obvious but equally important claim: even when formation fails—when a child breaks down in medical school, when a path proves destructive—the breakdown does not reveal what the child was called to. It reveals only what didn't work. The child who fails medical school might have been "called" to nursing, teaching, or nothing vocational at all—failure indicates cognitive limitations, psychological vulnerabilities, or mismatched capacities, not God's purposes. It may be that this very failure is part of how God forms the person toward His purposes—but that possibility only becomes visible in hindsight. Joseph at forty could look back and recognize God's purposes; at twenty, sold into slavery, he could not. Interpreting every formation failure as a violation of one's calling makes every formation failure evidence of parental malpractice. Parents need a criterion that operates during formation, not one that becomes clear only after.

None of this denies that God has purposes for John—or for any child. He does. But those purposes are typically revealed through faithfulness over time, not decoded in advance through the available indicators. The question for parents is not whether calling exists but whether it can guide formation decisions made years before it becomes clear. It cannot. And so parents need a different criterion—one by which to direct their children's formation—that can be observed during formation, tested against evidence, and adjusted when the evidence says they were wrong.

The fact that calling cannot ordinarily be known ahead of time reflects a deeper truth: The goal of human life is to glorify God, expressed through loving Him and neighbor, not finding and optimizing some inner self. The focus, then, should not be on discovering calling but on glorifying God through faithful obedience over time.

4

THE FOUNDATION

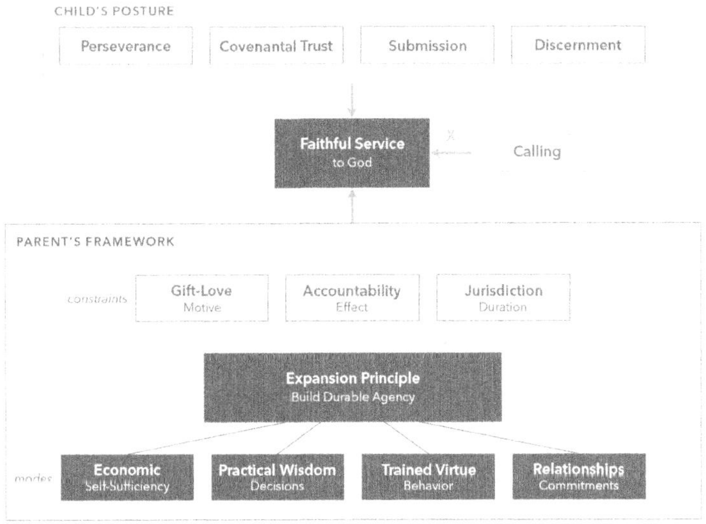

THE FRAMEWORK'S PURPOSE

The ultimate purpose of formation is spiritual: children who know and faithfully serve God across a lifetime. This is not one goal among several but the end toward which everything else is ordered. Economic success, practical competence, moral character, and healthy relationships matter because they enable faithful service—not as ends in themselves.

Faithful service to God does not require vocational ministry or extraordinary spiritual achievement. For most Christians across history, faithfulness has looked ordinary: providing for a household, raising children in the fear of the Lord, serving the local church, loving neighbors. Paul's instruction to the Thessalonians captures this: "Make it your ambition to lead a quiet life and attend to your own business and work with your hands, just as we commanded you, so that you will behave properly toward outsiders and not be in any need" (1 Thessalonians 4:11–12). Not burdening others is itself faithful stewardship. The parent who builds durable agency in a child—enabling that child to provide for a family, contribute to the church, and serve without requiring others' support—has equipped them for the kind of faithfulness that Scripture commends.

But parents cannot produce faith in their children. Faith is God's gift through the Spirit. What parents can do is build the capacities through which faith is usually expressed and sustained—while exposing children to Scripture, prayer, worship, and Christian community. This is where durable agency comes in. It is a concrete target that parents can actually aim at and assess.

DURABLE AGENCY DEFINED

Durable agency is the sustained capacity to direct one's own life. This is what formation aims to build. A teenager can make decisions, but only because parents provide the foundation—the money, the structure, the safety net. That's borrowed capacity, not built capacity. And a teenager can't yet do what adults must do: support aging parents, provide for a spouse and children, give generously to church and community. An adult with durable agency can act effectively across a lifetime—not just for themselves, but for others—without needing someone else to prop them up.

Durable agency comes in degrees. Someone with more resources, deeper wisdom, stronger character, and richer relationships has more of it than someone lacking these. It can't be measured precisely, but it is more concrete than calling—and that's what gives parents something to actually work with.

Durable agency is necessary for flourishing, but it doesn't guarantee it. Someone can have economic stability, practical wisdom, strong character, and deep relationships—and still lack joy, meaning, or closeness with God. The framework doesn't claim that building agency ensures a good life. It claims that without agency, sustained faithful service becomes structurally harder. The person who is broke, incompetent, or relationally isolated faces barriers to serving God and others that the person with agency doesn't face. Formation builds the platform. Grace supplies the meaning. A child formed toward durable agency who later wastes that capacity hasn't proven the formation was wrong—they've misused what was rightly built. The parent's job is to build capacity for faithful service. The adult child's job is to use it faithfully.

THE MODES OF DURABLE AGENCY

Durable agency is built through various modes, including: economic self-sufficiency, practical wisdom, trained virtue, and relational capacity. These are not the only modes, but they are central. They are the observable capacities that formation develops.

Economic self-sufficiency (income)—A person cannot act independently if they are financially dependent on others or one crisis away from ruin. Economic capacity creates the material foundation for choice.

Practical wisdom (decisions)—A person cannot make good decisions without judgment. The ability to discern what should be done in complex situations is essential to sustained self-direction.

Trained virtue (behavior)—A person cannot sustain independent action without self-control, courage, perseverance, and integrity. Character is not separate from agency; it is what makes agency durable. The person who lacks self-discipline, who cannot delay gratification, who breaks under pressure—this person's capacity for independent action cannot be sustained.

Relational capacity (relationships)—A person cannot act effectively in a social world without the ability to form and maintain commitments. Strong relationships expand options; destroyed relationships constrain even those with money and skills. Marriage, family, church, community—these require relational maturity that isolated individuals lack.

But these capacities must be understood fully—not as shallow, secular versions of themselves. Economic self-sufficiency isn't just earning money; it's stewardship for God's purposes. Practical wisdom goes beyond good judgment to judgment shaped by truth about God and reality. Trained virtue is more than good behavior—it is character formed by the Spirit that makes faithfulness natural. And relational capacity means not just social skill but the ability to keep covenants and serve others sacrificially. Each mode has a spiritual dimension that points toward its ultimate purpose.

Economic self-sufficiency is not one of four equal modes. It is the mode that most directly expands a person's options—the settings in which wisdom, virtue, and relationships can be put to work. A person without economic capacity may have all three in abundance but will face real limits on how far they can reach. This is not a statement about what matters most to God. It is a statement about how the world He made actually works. Scripture warns against loving money—it does not warn against having the ability to provide for one's household, support the church, and serve others from strength rather than dependence.

That primacy, however, does not mean economic capacity works alone. These modes work together. Formation that builds economic capacity while destroying character hasn't built durable agency—because the person can't sustain independent decision-making without virtue. Formation that builds wisdom while neglecting economic capacity leaves the person dependent on others' provision, no matter how wise their judgments might be.

Think of it as three levels. At the top: faithful service to God—the ultimate purpose. Beneath it: durable agency—the sustained capacity that makes faithful service possible. At the base: the modes—economic capacity, wisdom, virtue, relationships—which are the building blocks that parents actually develop.

Parents who confuse these levels will form poorly. Treating economic capacity as the goal rather than a tool misses the point. Believing that one can produce faith directly through enough effort confuses the parent's role with God's.

PHILOSOPHICAL GROUNDING

The modes of durable agency are not arbitrary. They reflect what philosophers have long recognized as the constituents of mature personhood.

Aristotle's account of human flourishing in the *Nicomachean Ethics*[5] describes an integrated vision: the capacity for genuine choice and self-direction, virtue formed through repeated right action until it becomes habit, the material resources necessary for virtuous activity, and practical wisdom developed through navigating real decisions. Thomas Aquinas[6] built on this foundation, emphasizing that virtue requires not just right action but transformed desire—the temperate person whose character has been reordered so that faithfulness is natural rather than forced. Alasdair MacIntyre,[4] in *After Virtue*, stresses that these capacities cannot be learned abstractly but only through sustained practice within demanding disciplines.

This tradition provides the grounding for the modes described above. Durable agency captures what these philosophers recognized: mature personhood is an integrated achievement, built through formation, not discovered pre-formed.

WHY VOCATIONAL DIRECTION IS THE PRIMARY LEVER

Parents have many tools for formation: modeling, teaching, discipline, exposure, conversation. But vocational direction—the choice of educational path, training, and career trajectory—is the primary lever because demanding paths build multiple modes at once.

The rigor itself is formative. A young man who resists enlisting but emerges from four years of military service with discipline, leadership capacity, and practical skills has been formed—not because he chose the path, but because the path built what he could not build on his own. The same is true of skilled trades, professional training, demanding academic paths, or entrepreneurship—each builds character, competence, and capacity together through sustained effort.

Consider a father who is a firefighter. He has spent decades in a profession that demands intense physical training, discipline, courage, and self-sacrifice. He makes split-second decisions that affect people's lives. He serves others daily—protecting their families, their homes, their livelihoods. Other careers might pay more. But taking all things into consideration, he believes this is a path that builds durable agency across every mode.

So he forms his son toward it. He brings him to the station. He teaches him about the job, making it real and exciting. He is deliberate about what he is building—not just career readiness but character.

This father has examined his motives honestly. He would feel genuine joy if his son became a teacher or an engineer. But every parent knows only a slice of the world, and this father knows firefighting. He believes—from decades of lived experience—that few paths build what this one builds. And he believes that the training itself will produce a man able to serve others out of love for what God has done for us.

This is why vocational direction receives such emphasis. Not only because economic capacity expands the most options, but because the path shapes character, wisdom, and capacity simultaneously. Parents who direct their children toward demanding vocational paths are not just building earning potential—they are using the most powerful lever available to build the whole person.

WHY DURABLE AGENCY RATHER THAN CALLING?

Chapter 3 argued that calling cannot reliably guide formation—it is unknowable before formation and cannot be decoded by failure after. So when a child claims to already know their calling, that claim—however sincere—doesn't outweigh the authority God has given parents to direct formation. Durable agency offers something parents can actually work with: observable markers like skill development, character growth, and relational health.

This difference matters practically. It frees parents from the impossible task of discerning God's hidden purposes and focuses them on building capacity. It frees children from measuring every hard moment against an imagined "true self." Both parent and child operate under uncertainty about ultimate calling, guided by what they can know: Is the capacity for self-directed life being built or destroyed?

A natural objection arises: if parents can observe the child's capacities—aptitudes, limitations, what they can and cannot sustain—have they not discerned at least part of the calling? The answer is no, because capacity and calling operate on different levels. Capacity reveals what someone can or cannot sustain, not God's purpose for them. A child who excels in biology may have capacity for medical school—but that is not the same as saying that medicine is their calling. Parents can see which doors are open or closed. They cannot see which door God intends them to walk through. Calling implies purpose—a direction toward which the child is designed. Capacity observation provides only boundaries within which many paths remain possible, and none is marked as "the one."

Even the Parable of the Talents, often cited to support ability-based calling discernment, makes this same distinction:

it demands stewardship, not a particular form of stewardship (Matthew 25:14–30). A child should develop what God has given. But developing a talent is not the same as building a life around it.

This does not mean that all paths are equal or that parents choose arbitrarily. Some paths reliably build multiple modes of durable agency simultaneously. Military service develops discipline, practical wisdom, economic capacity, and relational skill through sustained difficulty. A path that builds fewer modes, or builds them less reliably, represents a different formation bet—not a forbidden one, but one that requires justification.

WHY PARENTAL JUDGMENT?

Another objection arises: Why should parents be trusted to assess their child's capacity? The answer depends on what kind of claim parents are making.

When parents assess capacity, they are making judgments that can be tested: "Based on what I have seen, I think my daughter can handle law school." That judgment might be wrong—but it can be checked against reality and corrected when evidence piles up. A child with a mind for analytical thinking could serve God faithfully in medicine, law, engineering, research, finance, or a dozen other fields. What parents can see—their child's abilities and strengths—tells them which doors are open. It does not tell them which door God intends the child to walk through.

But why should parental judgment take precedence over the child's own view of their capacity? Because parents and children assess different things. The child knows what feels hard right now. The parent can better judge whether that difficulty means that the child cannot handle the path—or whether it is just the normal friction of demanding training. The twenty-year-old who resists biology often cannot tell the difference between "this is beyond me" and "this is hard and I do not like it"—a distinction that often only becomes clear years later. Parental authority exists precisely to make judgments children cannot yet make for themselves.

This includes children who feel called to ministry or missions. The framework does not forbid vocational ministry—it requires that durable agency be built first, absent direct revelation from God. A child who finishes nursing school and then enters missionary service has durable agency: she could support herself if circumstances required. She is choosing dependence from a position of strength, not fragility. The parent's job is to build capacity. The adult child decides how to use it. Formation aims to produce adults capable of choosing sacrifice—not adults for whom instability is the only option.

CALIBRATED TO CAPACITY

Durable agency looks different for each child. It is measured against what that specific child can achieve—not against some universal standard that applies to everyone.

For a child with significant cognitive limitations, durable agency might mean semi-independent living and meaningful contribution within their abilities. For children with learning disabilities, ADHD, autism, or other differences, the goals for durable agency must be adjusted to what they can actually handle. For a child born with physical disabilities, it might mean developing skills that fit their physical limits.

The test stays the same: Does formation expand this child's

future capacity to direct their own life—relative to where they started—or does it close off possibilities they actually have? A child pushed toward dental school who cannot sustain its demands experiences breakdown. A child with Down syndrome directed toward any employment experiences expansion. The same path can build agency for one child and destroy it for another. Parents must know their particular child.

Capacity is not always fixed. Sometimes it changes mid-formation through circumstances no one chose—the death of a family member, a sudden financial crisis, a medical diagnosis that reshapes everything, or a car accident that leaves permanent injury.

But not all suffering during formation is beyond the parent's control. Suffering caused by corrupt motives or ignored evidence of harm requires repentance. Suffering caused by poor judgment—the wrong path, an honest miscalibration—requires correction. God is sovereign over all of it, and grace covers parents who fall short.

When suffering is genuinely providential, the parent's response is not correction but trust. This is easy to write but agonizing to live. A parent watching their child suffer through something no one caused and no one can fix faces a kind of grief that no framework resolves. But even here, especially here, God is not absent. All suffering can form a child regardless of its source. Joseph was formed through his brothers' sin. David through Saul's.

Formation is not about building the best possible life. It is about knowing God and serving Him faithfully. A child who learns to trust God through a disease that will not go away is being formed in ways that no vocational path could replicate. So is the child who develops humility through limitation, or who grows in relational depth because suffering stripped away what was superficial.

None of this removes the grief. Even parents who believe that suffering serves God's purposes will find that the emotional pain does not always go away. Years later, a random moment—a song, a photograph, seeing another child at the playground—sends a parent to weep alone behind a closed door, because the grief never fully left. But even that ache serves a purpose—a constant reminder of the need for the gospel, for a Savior who suffered too, and for a world that is not yet what it will be. Parents who can receive providential suffering as God's sovereign work have not arrived at easy acceptance. They have arrived at the framework's deepest truth: faithful service to God sits above durable agency, not beneath it.

5

THE 1+3 FRAMEWORK

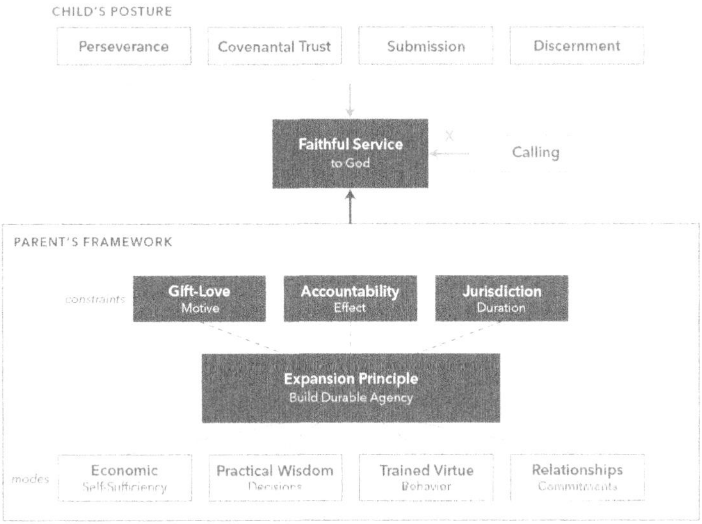

The framework rests on one governing principle, bounded by three constraints. The principle defines what formation should build. The constraints govern its motive, its effects, and its duration.

EXPANSION PRINCIPLE

This is the Expansion Principle: Formation is legitimate when it expands durable agency. This is the criterion by which any path should be evaluated. It asks a simple question: Does this expand the child's sustained capacity to direct their own life?

This sounds obvious—but notice what it's not. Not "what does the child want?" Not "what is the child called to?" Not "what worked for me?" The question is narrower and more testable: Does this path build capacity, or does it just feel right?

Most parents don't ask this question consistently. Some defer to the child's preferences—"she loves art, so we'll support art"—without asking whether art builds capacity or forecloses it. Others impose a path—"you'll join the family business"—without asking whether it serves the child or the parent's ego. The framework cuts through both errors with a single question: Does this build durable agency?

Different parents will answer that question differently—prioritizing different paths and modes based on their theology, culture, resources, and their particular child. For some families, formation means directing a child toward professional training. For others, it means skilled trades, military service, apprenticeships, agriculture, or entrepreneurship. For children with disabilities, it may mean independent living. All build durable agency; they differ in timeline, cost, and structure—not in value. The principle stays constant: expand future capacity. The framework does not adjudicate between these priorities. The specific path depends on what fits the family and the child.

This also means that the framework can critique decisions without telling parents what to choose. Directing a child toward law school for status violates gift-love—even if law school builds agency. Directing toward the Peace Corps but ignoring signs that the child is breaking down violates accountability. Keeping a child dependent indefinitely violates jurisdiction. The criterion stays the same. How parents apply it varies.

GIFT-LOVE CONSTRAINT

Chapter 2 established the distinction between gift-love (serving the child's good) and need-love (using the child to meet parental needs). Here is how it works as a check on parental motivation.

The Gift-Love Constraint requires that formation be motivated by the child's good—not by the parent's need for validation. Even when formation actually expands agency, it violates this constraint if the parent's motivation is corrupt. A parent who pushes their child toward a prestigious career because they need to prove something through their child's success has violated gift-love—even if the path builds durable agency. A good outcome doesn't justify a bad motive.

As Chapter 2 explored, need-love corrupts both directive and permissive parents and it often operates beneath the sur face. Parents must examine their motives with brutal honesty. Can they feel genuine joy if their child succeeds in a different field—or do they need them on this specific path? When their child struggles, is their first response concern for the child or anxiety about the outcome? Do they need their child to agree they made the right choice—or can they handle disagreement without getting defensive? If formation fails, will they see it as the child's lost opportunity or as their own failure? When their child resists, do they listen with curiosity or react like their authority is under attack? No parent acts from pure gift-love. But these questions reveal whether need-love has taken over.

Self-examination is rarely sufficient. The parent most

captured by need-love may be the one least able to recognize it on their own. That is why outside accountability is not just helpful—it is often necessary. Parents who question their own motives should seek honest input from people who know both them and their child. Not to confirm that they are on the right track, but to expose blind spots they cannot see themselves. The Gift-Love Constraint only works if parents have relationships where others can challenge them honestly.

Detecting need-love in one's own motivations doesn't mean that the formation path is automatically wrong—but it requires action.

First, parents must repent before God, acknowledging that they have been using their child to meet their own needs. Second, they must honestly reassess: Does this direction genuinely expand the child's agency, or did need-love distort their judgment from the start? Third, they should seek accountability by sharing their struggle with someone who knows both them and their child—need-love thrives in isolation but weakens when exposed to outside perspective. Finally, they must adjust whatever need-love has distorted. If it created excessive pressure, rigidity, or an inability to respond to evidence, those things must change—even if the overall direction stays valid.

The Gift-Love Constraint doesn't rule out difficult paths—it ensures that those paths serve the child rather than exploit them. Parents acting from gift-love can direct their children toward demanding training, maintain high expectations, and persist through resistance. What they cannot do is need the child's success, use the child to prove something, or refuse to adjust when evidence shows that their direction was wrong. The constraint governs motivation more than behavior. It addresses the *why* behind formation decisions—ensuring that even when parents exercise strong authority, they do so for the child's good rather than their own unmet needs.

ACCOUNTABILITY CONSTRAINT

Gift-love doesn't guarantee good judgment. Nearly every parent believes that their intentions are good. A parent can genuinely want their child's good and still unintentionally harm their child. The difference is what happens next. The gift-love parent can adjust when the path isn't working—because their identity doesn't depend on being right. The need-love parent can't adjust—because admitting that the path was wrong feels like admitting *they* were wrong. Legitimate formation requires ongoing responsiveness to evidence of systemic failure.

Parents have authority to direct children toward durable agency—even when the child initially resists or dislikes the path. Many children pushed through demanding training resist at first but later develop genuine engagement as competence grows or as they discover areas within the field that fit them. This is productive struggle, not breakdown. Many children won't jump at the chance to volunteer at a soup kitchen or hospital, preferring video games or time with friends; but through the experience, they may develop virtue. However, when formation produces persistent inability despite sincere effort, escalating psychological crisis, or patterns of breakdown, continued pressure becomes illegitimate. At that point, the parent is no longer building agency—they are destroying it.

Because the distinction between productive struggle and systemic breakdown determines whether continued direction is legitimate or harmful, parents need more than abstract categories. Productive struggle typically shows improvement over time, even if slowly. The child expresses frustration but keeps communicating. Difficulty stays contained—the struggle is in the demanding area, but the rest of life remains stable. The child may complain, but they still engage, and they recognize—even reluctantly—that they are growing.

Systemic breakdown looks different. It may show up academically (persistent failure despite effort), psychologically (escalating crisis requiring intervention), relationally (progressive destruction of the parent-child bond), or spiritually (hardening toward God, loss of faith connected to formation pressure). Difficulty persists or worsens despite sustained effort across multiple semesters. The child withdraws relationally—not just during conflict but as a pattern. Symptoms escalate: anxiety becomes debilitating, stress produces physical illness, sadness slides toward depression. Failure spreads beyond the formation domain into friendships, sleep, spiritual life, or self-care. Most tellingly, the child begins deceiving parents about performance or well-being—not from laziness but because honesty feels impossible.

When a child manages the parent's perception rather than sharing their reality, relational breakdown has already occurred regardless of grades. Timing also matters. One difficult semester is not breakdown; three years of declining function is. Parents should ask: Is this getting better, staying the same, or getting worse? When parents suspect systemic breakdown, outside counsel—from church leadership, physicians, or counselors—provides the external perspective that invested parents often cannot achieve alone.

Parents must also recognize that breakdown is often invisible until it becomes severe. If a child feels unable to tell their parent when they are struggling—if honesty feels impossible because the relational environment makes vulnerability unsafe—the formation has already failed the Gift-Love Constraint even if academic metrics remain positive. This means that the Accountability Constraint requires not only monitoring for observable symptoms but cultivating the relational safety that makes honest reporting possible. Parents should ask not only "Is my child showing signs of breakdown?" but "Would my child tell me if they were breaking down?" If the answer to the second question is uncertain, preventive action is warranted: church counsel, professional assessment, and proactive inquiry about the child's internal experience—not as surveillance but as care.

Parents should also attend to cumulative relational temperature, not just acute crisis moments. Formation damage often accumulates gradually—small withdrawals, slowly diminishing trust, conversations that become progressively more guarded. No single interaction triggers the Accountability Constraint, yet the aggregate does. A child who still passes classes but has grown distant over three years, who shares less each semester, who comes home but no longer confides—this pattern warrants attention even without dramatic breakdown. Parents who monitor only for crisis may miss the slower erosion that produces adult children who succeed professionally but describe their upbringing as something they survived rather than something that formed them.

The constraint is consequential, not precautionary: Parents need not prove in advance that their direction will work. They act on reasonable judgment about what builds durable agency, then adjust when evidence accumulates that they misjudged this child's capacity. A parent's moral culpability lies not in choosing an initially difficult path, but in persisting past the point where damage becomes clear. Parents remain accountable to God throughout the formation process and must continuously evaluate whether their approach is building or destroying agency.

But seeing that evidence clearly is harder than it sounds. The parent who pushes too hard wants their child to succeed. The parent who fails to push wants their child to be happy. The parent who cannot see breakdown wants their child to grow. Every one of them would say they are paying attention. What separates harmful formation from helpful formation is not good intentions, which almost all parents have, but wisdom, self-knowledge, and a willingness to respond to evidence.

Three obstacles make this harder than it sounds. First, formation requires mental and emotional energy—the ability to think carefully about direction, to engage conflict in a Christ-like manner, and to absorb a child's resistance without reacting poorly. Life competes for that energy. Work demands pile up, marriages require attention, health problems intrude, and the ordinary stress of daily life drains the tank. Parents who are too busy, too tired, or too depleted may find they have nothing left for the hard work of formation. They default to either rigid control (because careful discernment takes energy they lack) or passive drift (because engagement takes energy they lack). Neither serves the child.

Second, every person has blind spots—not a flaw to fix but a basic fact of being human. We do not know what we do not know, no matter how hard we try. Parents who genuinely act from gift-love, who watch carefully for breakdown, who sincerely want their child's good—these parents still cannot see everything. The very investment that makes them care deeply about their child also makes them unable to judge the situation with full clarity.

Third, everyone believes they are open to feedback. Everyone says they are willing to listen, willing to change, willing to consider other views. Everyone believes their decisions are reasonable—or at least more reasonable than others give them credit for. But saying it does not make it so. The parent most convinced of their own openness may be the least able to receive constructive criticism.

These three obstacles—depleted capacity, blind spots, and self-deception—explain why the Accountability Constraint rarely works well in isolation. Parents need outside perspective: people who can see what they cannot, who will speak honestly, and who know them well enough to distinguish real change from the appearance of change.

And not just any outside perspective. Parents need *diverse* outside perspective, including voices they expect to disagree with. Seeking counsel only from people who share their views produces agreement, not accountability. The parent who asks only friends who support rigorous formation will hear that rigor is good, while the parent who asks only friends who doubt parental authority will hear that direction is suspect. Neither provides real accountability. True outside perspective means seeking input from people who might challenge the parent's approach—the friend who thinks the chosen path is too demanding, the family member who worries the child seems unhappy, the church member who questions whether this path fits the child. These voices may be wrong, but dismissing them without serious thought suggests that the parent seeks support rather than truth.

This diverse perspective takes several forms. The church community—elders and pastors who know both parent and child—can ask hard questions about whether formation is building capacity or producing breakdown, and can observe relationship patterns and spiritual health that grades do not capture. Trusted friends and extended family often see what parents miss—the grandmother who notices that her grandchild has grown distant, the family friend who sees tension that the parents have gotten used to. Professionals offer objective assessment: counselors can evaluate mental health, doctors can identify physical signs of chronic stress, and teachers can assess whether academic struggle reflects real limits or temporary difficulty.

Parents who resist outside perspective should ask whether they are protecting their child or protecting their own judgment. The pattern matters here: parents who have dismissed multiple counselors, left churches that raised concerns, or cut off family members who asked hard questions should see this pattern itself as a warning sign. Cutting off outside voices is not wisdom—it is danger. When every external voice has been silenced, the parent has removed the very safeguards that this framework requires.

JURISDICTION CONSTRAINT

But when is the endpoint for parental authority and how should it be determined?

The civil marker uses the legal age of eighteen. But legal adulthood defines responsibility before the government, not spiritual authority within the family. And the number itself is newer than most people realize. The age at which parental authority ends has varied dramatically across history—from as young as eighteen in ancient Athens, to twenty-five in Roman civil law, to no age limit at all under Roman *patria potestas*, Confucian filial piety, and the Japanese *ie* system.

In the modern world, virtually every nation has settled on eighteen, but this agreement is remarkably recent. Until the late

1960s, twenty-one had been the Western standard for centuries. The shift to eighteen was triggered not by any finding about human development, but by a military argument—first made during World War II and finally successful during Vietnam—that those old enough to be drafted should be old enough to vote. The United States lowered its voting age in 1971,[7] states quickly lowered the age of majority to match, Europe followed through a 1972 Council of Europe resolution,[8] and the 1989 UN Convention on the Rights of the Child pushed the standard globally.[9] The number that virtually every modern parent takes for granted as the natural endpoint of their authority is less than sixty years old—and was adopted for political reasons entirely unrelated to when a child is actually formed. A biblical principle cannot rest on a government decision this recent and this arbitrary.

The other common positions at least try to use something more substantive. The educational marker uses college graduation as the dividing line. But this ties a biblical category to a modern school system. Not all children attend college—does a child who enters a trade at eighteen become an adult immediately while a classmate remains under authority for four more years? Those who pursue longer training graduate well into their late twenties. Are they still under parental authority at twenty seven? And the marker assumes a stable structure. College as a near-universal experience is recent in Western culture and is far from universal globally. A principle for when parental authority ends cannot depend on an institution that did not exist for most of human history and still does not exist everywhere today.

The economic marker draws the line at financial independence. But this puts too much weight on earning power alone. A sixteen-year-old with a part-time job earns income but is not an adult. A child could also rebel against parental direction and get a job specifically to claim independence—turning self-sufficiency into a tool for escaping authority rather than proof of readiness for it.

The self-assessment marker lets the child decide when he or she is ready. This position defeats itself. It lets the child decide when parental authority ends—but making that decision well requires the very maturity that parental authority exists to build. The child is grading their own test.

Each of these markers reflects something real—legal standing, education, earning power, self-knowledge. But none are rooted in Scripture. They are cultural habits, school timelines, economic benchmarks, or subjective self-assessments treated as though they were universal truths.

The covenantal marker is different. Every position on this question requires inference. The question is whether one infers from Scripture or from cultural convention. Scripture provides the foundation: children are commanded to obey their parents (Ephesians 6:1, Colossians 3:20), establishing that parental authority is not merely pragmatic but divinely ordained. Genesis 2:24 establishes that this authority has an endpoint: a child leaves father and mother to establish their own household. The parent's task is not perpetual control but preparation for the transition to independent adulthood. This much is clear from Scripture.

What requires inference is identifying that endpoint. Ephesians 6:1 and Colossians 3:20 command children to obey parents without age qualification, addressing children as members of a dependent household. Genesis 2:24 describes marriage as the moment of leaving and Scripture consistently places that transition under parental authority. Numbers 30 affirms parental authority over marriage. Furthermore, this is reaffirmed centuries later by the apostle Paul in 1 Corinthians

7:36–38, where he describes a daughter "past her youth" still subject to her father's authority.[14] The father in this passage is debating whether to give his daughter in marriage. Taken together, this framework reasons that parental authority extends until marriage.

But this principle requires constraints to prevent misuse. Parents have an obligation to actively facilitate marriage—not merely to wait passively or veto prospects without offering alternatives. A parent who demands high spiritual maturity, vocational stability, or particular character qualities cannot simply veto prospects; they must invest proportional effort to help the child encounter people who meet those criteria. Parents who prioritize vocational formation to the point of delaying marriage into their thirties or forties, or who discourage marriage to maintain authority, violate the purpose of this boundary. Passive veto authority without active facilitation is manipulation—extending parental authority indefinitely while claiming to seek quality.

This positive obligation—actively facilitating marriage once the child is ready—takes different forms across cultures and contexts. In some traditions this might mean formal matchmaking or engaging in discussions with other families about potential matches. In contemporary Western contexts it might mean expanding the child's social circles through church community, facilitating gatherings where suitable young people can meet, or making family connections available. In close-knit ethnic or religious communities, it might involve leveraging extended family networks or community leaders who know eligible young adults.

I acknowledge that this positive obligation is not directly commanded in Scripture—Genesis 2:24 describes marriage as a transition, not parental duties before it. I include it to close a loophole: without it, parents could extend authority indefinitely through passive veto. If multiple years pass, multiple reasonable prospects have been declined, and parents have made no effort to facilitate alternatives—this pattern suggests control, not lack of suitable options.

What constitutes "reasonable prospects" and "sufficient facilitation" will vary by community and context, and the framework cannot provide universal metrics. But the church has standing to intervene when the pattern becomes clear: a child ready for marriage at twenty-four who remains unmarried at thirty-two with a history of parental vetoes and no parental facilitation raises questions that the church should ask. This is a limitation that the framework cannot fully resolve through abstract criteria—it requires the community discernment that only a functioning church can provide.

For children who do not marry, parental directive authority should still appropriately end around the age when marriage would normally occur. The boundary exists to limit parental authority, not to be manipulated into extending it. The issue is not whether to form, but how to form legitimately within this time-bounded framework toward the ultimate goal: children who can know and faithfully serve God, exercising mature obedience and stewardship across their lifetime.

But there is a deeper question beneath all of this: what is the biblical status of an unmarried young adult who lives independently and no longer considers themselves subject to parental authority? Scripture nowhere explicitly treats it as a default category or a necessary stage in life.

Consider the assumed arc of human life. As a child, a person submits to parents. A single young adult submits to no one. In marriage, a person submits to a spouse. There is something incoherent about this narrative of submission, autonomy, submission, and that gap is not neutral. Over five, ten, or fifteen years of independence, a young adult who once practiced submission develops habits running in the opposite direction—prioritizing personal comfort, deciding without consulting anyone, treating autonomy as a right. These habits harden, and the person arrives at marriage unfamiliar with what daily submission actually looks like.

This is not a claim that singleness is inferior to marriage. Paul honors it in 1 Corinthians 7 and even prefers it for those with the gift. But Paul's singleness has a clear orientation: undivided devotion to the Lord (1 Corinthians 7:35). Freedom from marital obligations exists for greater service, not personal autonomy.

Most unmarried adults in their late twenties and thirties did not choose singleness as a calling. They arrived at it by default—unable to find a spouse, unsure how to pursue marriage, conditioned by a culture that treats indefinite delay as normal. When many say they are "content with singleness," they often mean they have learned to cope with an outcome they did not choose. A system that treats singleness as a default is resignation dressed in spiritual language. This is not a critique of single adults faithfully serving God and actively pursuing marriage. It is a critique of a system that does not actively support them.

This clarifies what the positive obligation to facilitate marriage is designed to prevent—not that a child might be called to single service, but drift into a state without practicing submission, without clear purpose, and without accountability beyond personal preference. The capacities required for marriage—capacities this framework addresses later—do not hold indefinitely without a structure that exercises them. The goal is not to force marriage but to ensure formation is aimed at something, and that parents do not passively allow their children to drift by failing to act.

HOW THE FRAMEWORK WORKS TOGETHER

Having established the three constraints individually, the question now is how they function together.

The Expansion Principle establishes formation's purpose: building durable agency that enables lifelong faithful service to God. But purpose alone cannot prevent abuse. These three constraints govern the internal (motive), external (effect), and temporal (duration) dimensions of parental authority.

These constraints need each other. Gift-love without accountability lets well-meaning parents destroy what they're trying to build. Accountability without jurisdiction produces parents who adjust well but never let go. Jurisdiction without either just puts a clock on bad parenting. Together, they keep parental authority real but bounded—strong enough to direct, honest enough to adjust, and temporary enough to end.

Parents act under uncertainty and may err despite faithfulness to these constraints. The question is not whether this framework removes uncertainty—it cannot—but whether it provides more concrete, observable criteria than the alternatives. When calling fails to guide a decision, the only answer is 'you didn't discern well enough'—with no way to identify what went wrong or what to do differently. When this framework identifies a failure, it traces to a specific constraint with observable evidence and a corrective path. It addresses the primary ways in which parental authority corrupts: when parents use children to meet their own needs, when they persist past evidence of harm, or when they refuse to relinquish authority after its season has passed. Formation conducted within these bounds serves the child's good while acknowledging parental fallibility.

That fallibility is the very reason church accountability is essential. The church's role is to hold parents accountable to the constraints—not to direct the specific formation path. The framework grants formation authority to parents (Ephesians 6:4), not to the church, and the church's scope is the health of the process, not the content of the decision. Elders who ask whether a parent is watching for breakdown are exercising legitimate pastoral care, but elders who tell parents which career their child should pursue have overstepped. The constraints are moral questions—motive, harm, and the duration of authority—and the church is equipped to evaluate moral questions. The specific formation path is a practical decision on which Scripture is silent, and the church has no authority to dictate where Scripture does not speak (Matthew 15:9). This distinction is deliberate: the family and the church hold different authorities over formation, and neither should absorb the other's role.

6

IMPLEMENTATION

WHAT FORMATION REQUIRES

The Expansion Principle establishes the criterion for legitimate formation, but what does formation actually require?

Many justify non-intervention or mild intervention—the belief that if parents avoid "imposing" their will, the child's God-given calling will naturally emerge. Reinforced by the cultural assumption that parental authority ends at eighteen or after college, this permissive approach often results in young adults who, by their mid-to-late twenties, are still unsettled—vocationally, relationally, or morally—and who lack the durable agency needed to establish households.

Formation is active, not passive. It does not consist merely of exposing children to options and allowing their interests to emerge. Research shows that permissive parenting—showing love but not setting demands or structure—leads to lower grades, weaker self-control, and worse financial outcomes in adulthood. Authoritative parenting—combining warmth with clear expectations and structure—produces better results.[10-13] But this research does not demonstrate that any specific vocational direction is optimal—the studies compare parenting styles, not particular formation paths. The framework's application to specific vocational direction is therefore an extension of the empirical principle, not a direct finding of the research itself.

A permissive parent might say: "I encouraged my child to take challenging courses, but they prefer art classes. I respect their choice." This framework says something different: "My child will complete calculus, chemistry, and physics—regardless of their preference for art." These build quantitative literacy and scientific reasoning that expand future options. Art remains available as an elective or lifelong pursuit, but the foundational disciplines are non-negotiable during formation.

Similarly, a permissive parent might say, "My daughter loves fitness and helping people with their health. She wants to become a fitness influencer and build an online coaching business. I respect her passion and her entrepreneurial drive." The framework would say: "While I respect her passion, I want my daughter to pursue physical therapy. It builds on the same love of fitness and the human body, but it produces a credential that provides economic stability for life—along with the wisdom that comes from making complex decisions under uncertainty, discipline under pressure, and relational maturity that demanding training develops. If she still wants to build an online fitness presence after she has her credential, she can—from a position of strength rather than fragility."

Another parent, applying the same framework to the same daughter, might say: "I want you to build this business—but I am going to structure how you build it. You will write a real business plan. You will manage real finances with your own money, not mine. You will hit revenue benchmarks we agree on together, and if the business is not self-sustaining within two years, you will pivot to a credentialed path. The business is the goal—but the discipline is non-negotiable." This parent believes the agency built through the entrepreneurial process—learning to manage finances, build systems, recover from failure, and make decisions under uncertainty—outweighs the economic risks, provided the path is directed rather than left to drift.

In each of these cases, the pattern is the same. The permissive approach—assuming that if parents avoid "imposing," the child's capacities will naturally develop—systematically underestimates the role of discipline, constraint, and directed effort in building durable agency. The framework does not claim that the opposite choice is necessarily wrong. A parent who evaluates art or fitness coaching against the modes of durable agency and genuinely concludes that it builds sufficient capacity for their particular child has applied the framework—they have simply weighted the modes differently. Nor does the framework require that parents direct toward one specific path. Some parents will select a single direction they believe best builds capacity. Others will identify several paths that satisfy the Expansion Principle and give the child a choice among them. Both are legitimate exercises of parental authority. What the framework requires is that the decision be a conscious judgment about what builds durable agency, not a default to the child's preference.

Three reasons why active direction is typically necessary: First, durable agency requires competence in areas that children may not naturally choose. A child drawn to creative writing may resist formal logic or economics. A child drawn to engineering may resist communication and leadership development. Children naturally gravitate toward what interests them—but interest alone does not determine what builds durable agency. If formation only follows interest, children may avoid the very disciplines that build lasting capacity.

Second, intrinsic motivation can follow competence rather than preceding it. A child directed into competitive swimming may initially resist the early morning practices and physical discomfort. But as competence develops—as they see improvement, earn recognition, experience the satisfaction of mastery—resistance often transforms into genuine engagement. The child who resists anatomy coursework at twenty but thrives as a physical therapist at thirty has not "found their calling"—they developed the skill first, and then purpose followed. Formation can shape preferences; it does not merely discover them. To exclude this possibility would be to limit future agency.

Third, twenty-year-olds lack the wisdom to evaluate what builds long-term capacity. They can assess what feels aligned in the present, but they cannot reliably judge what will expand agency at forty. Parents bear responsibility to make decisions that children cannot yet make for themselves.

This means that parents must sometimes be direct despite

resistance. The Expansion Principle does not justify any parental preference, but it does justify structured direction toward paths that reliably build capacity, even when children initially resist. The test is whether formation expands future agency, not whether it aligns with present preference. Structure in formation is not the enemy of agency—it is the precondition for it.

Parents who direct formation are responsible for matching that direction with resources—counting the full cost of what they direct, including debt, time, and delayed household formation. For some families, significant educational debt may be the price of generational transformation: a family without professional income that produces a licensed professional has built durable agency across generations, even if debt is part of the cost. For other families, directing a child toward an expensive path while having the resources to pay—but choosing not to—shifts the cost of parental authority onto the child. The framework does not demand the most rigorous path available. It demands the most rigorous path the family can faithfully sustain.

Consider a sixteen-year-old daughter who loves literature and wants to major in English. If her parents believe that literature builds less durable agency—regardless of whether they are objectively correct—they might direct her toward law and fund her education, while allowing literature as a minor or lifelong pursuit. They explain: legal training combined with analytical thinking creates more options at forty. They provide exposure: internships, mentors in both fields. If she thrives in law despite initial resistance, formation is working. If she experiences systemic breakdown (failing despite sincere effort, escalating distress, inability to master material), the Accountability Constraint is triggered, and parents adjust, guiding the daughter into a different field that increases durable agency. But mere preference for literature does not override parental judgment about what builds agency.

WHAT ABOUT PASSION?

Could a child pursuing their passions also reach durable agency at forty? Some do—but a strategy is not validated by its best outcomes. It is validated by what it reliably produces. For every artist who builds financial stability, many remain economically fragile. Moreover, passion-first formation often depends on privilege many families cannot provide. A family struggling to make ends meet cannot afford to treat passion pursuits as anything but a luxury. The structured approach does not foreclose passion—it creates the foundation from which passion pursuits become sustainable. Structure preserves options; drift often forecloses them.

A daughter with artistic talent who builds durable agency through nursing does not lose her art. She gains the stability to use it freely—teaching free art classes to low-income children, serving her church's ministry through design, or mentoring young artists in her community. The talent is stewarded, not abandoned. It is deployed from strength rather than gambled on as a livelihood.

Some parents point to successful outcomes without active direction: "We let our children follow their interests, and they became an engineer and a successful business owner." As Chapter 1 discussed, this reasoning fails: survivorship bias, unrecognized formation, and the impossibility of knowing whether success came from the approach or despite it. Parents who understand what they are doing can adjust when circumstances require it. Parents who do not recognize their own influence have no framework for correction when things go wrong.

But intentional direction raises its own challenge: What about paths that seem to require giving up options? Some vocations—missionary work, pastoral ministry—appear to demand economic sacrifice rather than economic building. Does the framework rule these out?

It does not. The framework sequences them rather than forbidding them. A young adult who has built durable agency and then chooses to live on missionary support exercises mature stewardship. This differs fundamentally from a child who drifts into economic fragility because formation never built capacity. The missionary who could practice optometry but chooses to serve unreached people has options. The adult who never developed marketable skills has only constraints.

Consider a son with real athletic talent and a heart for missions. His parents direct him toward a Division I program—not because they are chasing a professional contract but because they believe the path builds durable agency across multiple modes at once. The physical demands build discipline and perseverance. Balancing a full course load with training and travel builds the capacity to perform under competing pressures. Team dynamics build relational maturity. The scholarship eliminates debt. The parents require the degree because the degree provides future options. The sport is the vehicle that builds character while the degree gets built.

He graduates with a degree and the discipline of someone who woke up at five every morning for four years. He plays professionally for two or three years. The income builds financial margin. The professional environment builds maturity under pressure at a level most twenty-three-year-olds never encounter. Then he steps away and enters missionary work—not from fragility but from strength. He has a degree. He has savings.

He has discipline built through years of physical and academic demand. If circumstances change, he has a degree, financial margin, and the discipline to pivot into any number of careers. His missionary service is a deployment of durable agency, not an escape from building it.

His parents did not chase the contract. They directed a path that used their son's talent and interest as the vehicle for building capacity. The sport served the framework.

Some readers will object: Didn't the disciples leave their nets immediately when Jesus called? They did—but they responded to a direct, personal command from Jesus, not an inner conviction, however strong. That kind of extraordinary revelation is not the norm for vocational discernment. Even Jesus did not begin his public ministry until he was thirty. The Son of God spent decades in obscurity—learning a trade, living under authority, building the ordinary capacities of adult life—before the work for which He came.

For everyone else, the principle holds: build capacity first, then deploy it for kingdom service—including radical deployment if that is where God leads. A genuine calling to missions, if real, will survive the years required to build durable agency. If it does not survive, it was not the kind of calling that warranted forgoing formation in the first place.

More fundamentally, it is the parent, not the child, who evaluates whether following passion serves durable agency. Some parents may discern that their child's passion, combined with exceptional talent and family resources, genuinely builds toward durable agency. Others may judge that passion pursuit risks economic fragility that burdens both child and future generations. Both represent parental authority exercised through the Expansion Principle. The child's preference does not determine the answer; the parent's evaluation does. The framework provides the criteria; parental authority determines the application.

But wise parents do not ignore what they observe. A child who lights up around animals, who spends hours building things, who gravitates toward music or numbers—these are real observations that parents should strongly consider when choosing a formation path. The parent who nurtures a daughter's love of design by directing her toward architecture has combined the child's interest with the broader perspective only a parent can provide. The child sees what she enjoys today. The parent sees what will build capacity for decades. When a child's passion aligns with a path that builds durable agency, nurturing that passion is not a concession. It is wise formation. The framework does not reject a child's interests. It rejects the assumption that interests alone should drive the decision, or that a child's passion reveals a calling the parent is obligated to follow.

WHAT ABOUT FAILURE?

Active formation does not mean shielding children from all failure. Some failures are formative—they teach consequences, build resilience, and develop the capacity to recover. The question is not whether to allow failure, but whether the failure builds or destroys durable agency.

A failure that builds durable agency has clear limits. The teenager who fails a test learns to study; the consequence is contained and the child moves forward stronger. The young adult who overspends and cannot make rent learns budgeting through discomfort rather than lecture. These failures hurt, but they teach. The child emerges with greater capacity, not less.

A failure that destroys durable agency forecloses future

options. The adult who drifts through their twenties without building capacity faces barriers that formative failures never create. The young person who accumulates debt for a credential that builds nothing arrives at thirty with constraints rather than options. These failures do not instruct—they cripple.

Parents differ in how much failure they will allow. Consider a teenager who wants to drive recklessly—speeding, skipping seatbelts, or texting behind the wheel. One parent takes the keys away. Another allows the teenager to drive, believing that a firsthand experience of receiving a speeding ticket or fender-bender will teach better than words. A third permits driving but installs a tracking app and sets clear consequences for violations.

Or consider a longer-term case. A child wants to pursue a path the parents believe is foolish—say, an unstable career with little economic prospect. Some parents will direct firmly toward a higher-agency alternative. Others will allow the attempt, believing that experiencing the consequences firsthand will teach what lectures cannot. Both approaches can reflect gift-love. The first parent prioritizes preventing foreseeable hardship. The second prioritizes the formation that comes through lived experience.

None of these parents is necessarily wrong. Where each parent draws the line will differ. Family culture, risk tolerance, the child's temperament, and theological convictions all shape that threshold. The framework does not adjudicate these differences. It provides a criterion: does this failure build or destroy the child's capacity for faithful service?

But wherever parents draw the line, the framework requires that they actively form through failure—not passively watch it play out. Allowing a child to fail is not the same as abandoning them to failure. The parent who permits costly consequences still has work to do afterward: helping the child understand what happened, why it happened, and what it means going forward. This is where the real work of formation happens. Watching a child suffer is painful. What makes it bearable is knowing that the suffering serves a purpose—the child is being built up, not just hurt. Too often, parents allow the failure but treat the rebuilding as an afterthought.

A child who fails and is helped back up learns that failure is survivable and that someone believes they can recover. A child who hears only "I told you so" learns that failure earns contempt and that struggling alone is safer than asking for help. The goal is not to protect children from all failure. The goal is to build them back up when failure comes. Often, the hardest failures—when met with rebuilding rather than lecturing—produce the deepest formation.

PRUDENTIAL CONSIDERATIONS

While parents possess authority to direct their children even over initial resistance, wise parents rarely need to resort to bare demands. Formation works best when it cultivates understanding and builds intrinsic motivation alongside competence. This might involve helping the child understand why a path builds durable agency, providing early exposure to what the work actually involves, connecting them with mentors who model the profession, or creating opportunities for the child to experience competence and recognition in the field. When children understand the purpose of formation and experience growing capability, resistance often transforms into engagement—not because their initial preferences were right, but because competence generates its own satisfaction.

However, the moral legitimacy of parental direction does

not depend on successfully generating enthusiasm. A parent who has clearly explained the rationale, provided reasonable exposure, and still faces resistance has not thereby lost their authority to proceed, provided that the formation still meets the Expansion Principle and Accountability Constraint.

Prudential considerations may also involve giving the child greater voice in formation decisions. The goal of formation is independence—a child who can direct their own life. This means that wise parents increasingly delegate decision-making to the child as competence and maturity grow. This includes, for some families, allowing the child to pursue a passion—not because the child demanded it, but because the parent judged it to be consistent with building durable agency. But the decision to delegate is itself a parental decision. The parent who evaluates a seventeen-year-old's judgment, track record, and maturity and concludes "she is ready to choose her own path" is exercising authority, not surrendering it. The parent who says "it's her life, it's not my place to direct her" without that evaluation has abdicated. Both produce the same outcome—the child chooses. But the first is a formation decision made from authority. The second is a vacuum. The framework endorses the first and challenges the second. The child does not decide when the child is ready. The parent does.

7

FORMATION BEGINS YOUNG

The framework addresses vocational formation—the direction of educational and career paths. But the capacities that make vocational formation possible do not appear suddenly at age sixteen. They are built across childhood.

This does not mean parents must map out their child's career at age five. It means that the modes of durable agency—economic capacity, practical wisdom, trained virtue, and relational capacity—have roots that grow long before vocational decisions arise. The teenager who can sustain demanding training was not born with that capacity. It was built through years of facing difficulty, completing hard tasks, and learning that effort produces results.

DEPTH MATTERS

Most parents teach their children some version of perseverance, discipline, and responsibility. The question is not whether these values get taught but how deeply they are internalized.

The Olympic skier and the recreational skier practice the same sport. But the Olympic athlete who trained four hours daily for a decade built a fundamentally different body, a different set of habits, a different capacity for sustained effort. What appears as natural talent is usually deep formation that began early and continued long. The recreational skier learned to ski. The Olympic athlete built the capacity to sustain effort through years of difficulty—a capacity that transfers far beyond the slopes.

This distinction matters because demanding vocational formation requires deep foundations.

Consider two teenagers in high school. One spent childhood in structured activities with real consequences, worked part-time, and consistently met high academic expectations. The other learned the same values, but less deeply—activities continued until they became inconvenient, academic expectations stayed moderate, and difficulty was something to manage rather than something to master. Both teenagers "learned" discipline and perseverance. Their parents would say they taught these values. But only one has built the foundation that produces higher durable agency—not just career readiness, but increased capacity for faithful service to God across a lifetime.

WHERE DEPTH GETS BUILT

Depth can be built through many activities—competitive sports, demanding musical training, rigorous academics, age-appropriate work. The specific activity matters less than the structure: sustained effort over years, obstacles built into the path, clear feedback on performance, and real consequences for failure.

Consider four different paths. A child begins piano at age five, practices daily without exception even during the seasons when she begs to quit, performs in recitals where mistakes have consequences, pushes through the plateau where progress feels invisible, and by high school wins regional competitions. Another joins a swim team at age eight, wakes up for practices at five in the morning regardless of how he feels, competes in swim meets, and continues through years of marginal improvement before competing in state and national competitions. A third struggles with math in fourth grade, enrolls in a rigorous after-school program, fails problems repeatedly, learns to adjust, and by eighth grade tests into advanced courses. A fourth begins working at a family business at twelve, stocking shelves and serving customers, learns that showing up late affects others, that customers don't adjust to bad moods, and by high school manages weekend shifts independently.

These paths look nothing alike. But the structure is the same: sustained effort over years, obstacles built into the path, clear feedback on performance, and real consequences for giving up. The capacity to persevere was built not by the activity itself, but by how it was pursued.

WHAT THIS LOOKS LIKE

Consider Ava, a seven-year-old who plays competitive soccer. Like many kids, she enjoys it and wants to be good, but hard work is foreign to her. What matters is not the sport itself but what soccer is building. Ava's parents plan out a schedule: she wakes up at six every morning to run drills before school, trains in group settings three times a week, and plays against older, bigger kids who outmatch her physically.

This is a heavy schedule for a child her age. She does not always want to go to practice—she just got home from school, she just wants to play at home. She goes anyway. Not because her feelings do not matter, but because the capacity to follow through when motivation fades is more important than any single practice. She is learning that commitment does not depend on how she feels in the moment.

Ava plays in a game and the ball hits her directly in the face. She cries and wants to quit. But she is coached. She is encouraged. She goes back in. That decision—to return to something that just hurt her—builds something in her that will matter long after soccer is over.

What is being built through this process is not soccer skill. It is the capacity to push through difficulty, to submit to a structure she did not choose, to manage a schedule that stretches her, and to recover when something goes wrong. These capacities are transferable. The seven-year-old who learns to get back up after being hit in the face is building the same muscle she will need at twenty-two when a graduate program becomes overwhelming, or at thirty-five when marriage requires sustained sacrifice through a hard season. Whether soccer is the vehicle or something else entirely does not change the principle: formation that builds these capacities early creates the foundation that later formation requires.

Compare this to a child who plays recreational soccer once a week, or switches to a new sport every season. The child is having fun—and that may be what the parent is prioritizing. But the capacity to push through difficulty is not being built. When vocational formation arrives, the foundation will not be there.

None of this requires that she play soccer forever. As Ava grows, more of these decisions will shift to her. A wise parent increasingly delegates as competence and maturity develop. By ten, a parent may say, "you can quit soccer, but you must pursue another team sport with equal or greater rigor." By sixteen, the choice may broaden further—academic teams, part-time work, or starting a business. But at seven, the parent decides. And the child learns to move forward under that decision. The transfer of authority is gradual and earned, not sudden and assumed.

But this must be held in tension with the Accountability Constraint. If Ava's schedule began producing persistent anxiety rather than manageable stress—if she stopped sleeping, began dreading every practice with escalating distress rather than ordinary reluctance, or started withdrawing from relationships—the formation would need adjustment. Productive struggle builds capacity. Systemic breakdown destroys it. The parent who cannot tell the difference will push a child past her limits and ultimately reduce her capacity for faithful service to God.

CAPACITY FOR PERSEVERANCE

Parents sometimes worry about pushing too hard on young children. This concern is valid when pushing produces the systemic breakdown that the Accountability Constraint addresses. But the opposite error is more common: parents who protect children from difficulty, who remove obstacles before children encounter them, who treat comfort as the goal. These children arrive at adolescence without the capacity to handle demanding formation—not because they lack ability, but because the capacity was never built.

The damage is worse than it appears. Parents who let children quit when work becomes difficult are not merely failing to build capacity—they are removing their children precisely when growth would occur. Consider weightlifting: muscle growth happens in the final repetitions—the ones that hurt, the ones the body resists. A person who stops when the weight becomes uncomfortable never reaches the repetitions that actually build strength. The effort was real but produced little.

Parents who let children exit activities at the first sign of discomfort make the same mistake. They believe they are being responsive. Year after year of this pattern produces a teenager who has tried many things but built little—not because the activities lacked value, but because the child never stayed long enough to reach the repetitions that matter.

This is not an argument for ignoring genuine breakdown—the Accountability Constraint exists precisely to distinguish productive struggle from harm. But discomfort is not breakdown. Complaints, frustration, and resistance are normal responses to demanding formation; escalating crisis, persistent inability, and progressive deterioration are not. Confusing them in either direction—treating normal resistance as breakdown, or treating genuine breakdown as resistance—produces either a child removed from growth or a child destroyed by pressure. Neither outcome serves the child's good.

CAPACITY FOR SUBMISSION

But persistence through difficulty is not the only capacity that must be built early. Children must also learn to move forward despite disagreement—and this is a different muscle. A child might push through a hard swim practice because she wants to compete, yet refuse to continue piano because her parents require it. The first is persistence through chosen difficulty. The second is acceptance of direction despite conflicting preferences. These two capacities are often confused. A child with impressive persistence in chosen pursuits may still lack the capacity to accept direction when preferences conflict. Both capacities matter for vocational formation, but the second is often neglected.

Consider two teenagers: Teen A taught herself guitar over two years—practicing daily, learning songs by ear, performing at open mics. But when parents require continued piano lessons, she argues, stalls, and eventually shuts down.

Teen B shows moderate persistence in activities she enjoys. But when parents require violin practice she dislikes, she completes it without enthusiasm but without rebellion.

Teen A has more raw persistence. Teen B has more capacity for submission. When vocational formation arrives—when parents direct their child toward engineering, whether through explicit instruction or firm expectation—which teenager can receive that direction? This is why the distinction matters. Parents who see impressive grit in self-chosen activities may assume that their child is ready for directed formation. They are often wrong. The child who excels at what they chose may collapse when required to pursue what they did not choose.

Developing this capacity requires scaffolding. A basketball coach teaching a child to shoot does not start by saying, "Shoot the ball." The coach stands beside the child, physically guiding the elbow into position, adjusting the wrist, even supporting the ball during the release. The next week, the coach still corrects form but no longer holds the elbow—just taps it as a reminder. A month later, the coach watches from a few feet away, offering occasional verbal cues. Eventually, the coach says nothing at all. The child shoots with proper form because the external support has been internalized. The coach scaffolded: providing heavy structure at first, then progressively removing it as the child's capacity grew.

Developing the capacity for submission works the same way. Children must learn to move forward despite disagreement—and this capacity must be built incrementally, through years of practice on small things. A five-year-old learns to eat vegetables even when she would rather have dessert. A twelve-year-old attends the family gathering instead of staying home with friends, even when he sees no point in going. An eighteen-year-old pursues an engineering major even when she believes that music better reflects who she is. Each instance builds the muscle for accepting parental direction when the child disagrees. As children mature, their capacity for genuine disagreement matures with them. The five-year-old exhibits preference; the twelve-year-old exhibits reasoning; the eighteen-year-old exhibits principle. What remains constant is the pattern: voice the disagreement, then move forward under authority.

Parents who skip this training—who avoid conflict, who negotiate every decision, who let children opt out whenever they resist—find themselves facing an impossible situation when formation requires direction on something significant. But parents who demand blind obedience without ever permitting disagreement make the opposite error. They keep the training wheels on indefinitely—the child complies, but only because the parent still holds the bike. Neither child has learned to obey despite disagreement—one was never required to obey, the other was never allowed to disagree. Expecting a child to accept parental authority over college or career choices without this training is like expecting a leap from basic addition to calculus. The prerequisite steps were never built.

But what does genuine submission look like? A child who faces unwanted direction can respond in two ways: Do they obey? And do they stay relationally connected? This creates four possible responses.

	RELATIONALLY ENGAGED	RELATIONALLY WITHDRAWS
COMPLIES	Submission	Capitulation
REFUSES	Rebellion	Passive Resistance

Rebellion is refusing to obey while staying engaged—the child fights openly, hurting the relationship to protect their independence. *Passive resistance* is refusing to obey while withdrawing—the child shuts down, neither obeying nor connecting. *Capitulation* is obeying while withdrawing—the child does what they're told but gives up their voice to keep the peace. *Submission* is obeying while staying engaged—the child shares their disagreement, listens to the parent's reasoning, and moves forward under direction while staying relationally present.

Submission is what formation requires. A child who has only ever experienced the other three postures has no framework for healthy engagement with authority. When vocational or marriage direction arrives, they will likely withdraw, disengage, or escalate into relationship-damaging conflict.

What is being built through this process is a simple distinction that many children never learn: what one wants to do and what one should do are not the same thing. Sometimes they align. Sometimes they do not. Wisdom is knowing which situation one faces—and acting rightly regardless of preference. A child who never learns this distinction becomes an adult who cannot subordinate desire to duty, who interprets every unwanted obligation as oppression, and who lacks the basic capacity for faithfulness when faithfulness is costly.

CONNECTION TO VOCATIONAL FORMATION

Early formation does not determine vocational direction—it creates the capacity that makes direction possible. The child who arrives at age sixteen having built both the capacity for perseverance and for submission is prepared for a demanding vocational formation. The child who arrives having been protected from difficulty lacks the raw material that vocational direction shapes.

Parents who begin thinking about formation only when college applications loom have missed the most formative years. The teenager who resists demanding training because it is "too hard" may be revealing not a mismatch with the path but a gap in early formation. At that point, parents face a harder task: building foundational capacity while simultaneously directing vocational path.

This is why formation cannot wait. The practices that build durable agency must begin years before vocational decisions arise. Parents who invest in early formation create children capable of sustaining the demanding paths that build it. Parents who defer formation until adolescence often find the window for building foundational capacity has partially closed.

8

FORMATION AND DAUGHTERS

Some complementarian families form sons rigorously while forming daughters permissively, believing that this reflects biblical theology—it contradicts it. Formation that produces dependence rather than agency does not prepare a daughter for biblical submission—it prevents it. The result, in varying degrees, is wives less equipped to manage complex households, less able to steward resources wisely, less prepared to educate their children effectively, and more dependent on their husbands for spiritual growth. This is not biblical womanhood; it is dependence confused with submission.

WHY DAUGHTERS REQUIRE DURABLE AGENCY

The opening claim requires defense: why does permissive formation of daughters contradict complementarian theology rather than reflect it? Because the roles themselves require durable agency. Biblical complementarity functions only between two capable adults. Managing a household well requires patience, perseverance, critical thinking, problem-solving, and efficiency—precisely the capacities that rigorous formation develops. A wise mother can discern truth, teach her children effectively, offer counsel to her husband, and serve the church. Scripture honors such women: Abigail's wisdom saves lives when she intervenes with David (1 Samuel 25), Deborah leads Israel with judgment and courage (Judges 4), and older women are commanded to teach younger women how to live wisely (Titus 2:3–5). None of this wisdom emerges from intellectual complacency. It is built through the same rigorous formation that builds durable agency in sons.

SUBMISSION REQUIRES DURABLE AGENCY

Submission requires the capacity to disagree wisely, to offer genuine counsel, and to execute decisions effectively. A wife who cannot think critically or lacks the competence to evaluate decisions is not positioned for biblical submission—she is positioned for dysfunction.

Consider the difference. A wife without this capacity faces

her husband's decision with only three options: capitulation, rebellion, or passive resistance. None of these are biblical submission. Capitulation is dependence wearing submission's clothes. Rebellion is conflict justified as "having a voice." Passive resistance is disengagement disguised as peace. When these patterns take root in a marriage, they distort God's design for the relationship and breed dysfunction that compounds over years.

A wife with durable agency and the practiced capacity for submission has a fourth option: she engages fully, then defers willingly. She can say, "I see it differently, and here's why"—and her counsel has weight because she has the competence to evaluate the situation. When her husband decides otherwise, she can move forward without resentment—not because she lacks opinions, but because she learned long ago that what one wants and what one does are not always the same thing. Her submission is a choice, not a default. It is the exercise of agency, not its absence.

A common criticism of complementarianism is that submission produces dependence, not flourishing. Where that criticism applies, this framework agrees; however, the problem is not submission itself but formation that never builds the agency submission requires. The solution is not to abandon complementarian theology but to form daughters who can fulfill it from strength rather than collapse into it from weakness.

EQUAL RIGOR, EQUAL FORMATION

The framework requires parents to exercise the same formative authority toward daughters as sons. The Expansion Principle, the Accountability Constraint, and the time-bounded authority all apply equally. A daughter will complete physics and economics classes regardless of preference, for the same reason a son will.

Equal rigor does not require identical paths—a son directed toward engineering and a daughter directed toward nursing have both received demanding formation that builds durable agency. What the framework prohibits is the assumption that daughters need less because they will "just" be homemakers. The capacities developed through rigorous training—disciplined thinking, sustained effort under pressure, complex decision-making—prepare a daughter for the role God ordains.

Nor does equal formation mean identical deployment afterward. How a woman stewards her durable agency will vary based on circumstances the framework cannot anticipate. A mother of five navigating tight finances faces different demands than a mother of one with abundant resources. Some women—particularly in immigrant families—must work to put food on the table or to move their families to safer environments. Others find that their capacities allow them to serve faithfully through both career and household—and their families flourish under that arrangement. Still others devote themselves fully to household management because their families are best served by that dedication.

Income is the mode that most expands options, but it is not the only way durable agency is exercised. A woman who stays home but exercises practical wisdom, trained virtue, and deep relational capacity has not failed to deploy her formation—she has deployed it differently. The mother who teaches her children, manages a complex household, counsels her husband, and serves her church is exercising durable agency even if she earns no paycheck. The framework measures faithful stewardship, not income.

The framework does not adjudicate between these outcomes. It does not say "women should work" or "women should stay home." It says that durable agency is required—and how that agency is deployed depends on the family, the season, and the specific situation. What matters is the heart and the priority: Are her choices flowing from rightly ordered loves, or from disordered desires? Is she stewarding her capacity for faithful service, or pursuing career achievement as an end in itself? Is she serving her household, or escaping it?

OBJECTION: "RIGOROUS FORMATION CHANGES HER DESIRES"

If a daughter invests years in demanding professional training, builds competence, earns recognition, and develops an identity around achievement, she may not want to "give it up" for homemaking. Formation shapes desires—this is precisely what the framework claims. So will rigorous formation not shape her desires away from the roles complementarians honor?

The concern follows a logical thought process, but it confuses the goal of professional training. Whether for sons or daughters, the ultimate purpose of formation is faithfulness to God—and through that faithfulness, a desire to honor and work within God's design for marriage and family. A daughter who pursues professional training as an end in itself has missed the purpose. But this failure lies in the framing, not the training, which is where parental guidance comes in.

The concern also assumes that interest in demanding work and interest in homemaking are mutually exclusive. They are not. Homemaking does not preclude working, and capability in one domain does not eliminate desire for the other. Humans are complex beings with many interests at varying levels. A daughter can genuinely desire both meaningful professional contribution and faithful household management—just as the Proverbs 31 woman engaged in trade, production, and investment while watching over the affairs of her household.

The discipline is ensuring that these interests are rightly ordered. Because of our understanding of the gospel and what Christ has done for us, our priorities align with His. This does not mean that a daughter cannot have professional interests. It means those interests must be ordered under her primary commitments—to God, to her husband, to her children. A daughter formed with this ordering can pursue demanding training without that training competing with her future roles. The training serves the roles rather than displacing them.

OBJECTION: "RIGOROUS FORMATION DELAYS MARRIAGE"

The issue here is how one defines readiness. The framework's goal is durable agency for faithful service to God, with parental jurisdiction ending at marriage. If rigorous formation delays marriage indefinitely, formation has defeated its own purpose. But demanding formation does not necessarily mean indefinite delay. Nursing, teaching, or skilled work can be completed by the early twenties. Medicine and law take longer, but even these have clear endpoints. The question is not whether a daughter is currently earning income but whether she is on a defined trajectory with a foreseeable conclusion. A daughter in medical school is not "unready" for marriage—she is mid-formation with a clear end date. Some delay may even be preferable: a daughter who marries at twenty-six with durable agency is better positioned than one who marries at twenty-one without it. This decision rests with the parents whom God has placed in authority over their child. The framework provides a method for reasoning through such choices—it does not dictate the outcome.

And outcomes will vary, because capacity varies. Some daughters can handle demanding training alongside the serious pursuit of marriage; others cannot. The framework does not require the longest or most demanding path—it requires rigorous formation calibrated to the child.

The deeper error is treating formation and marriage preparation as sequential rather than parallel. A daughter pursuing rigorous training can simultaneously develop relational maturity, participate in church community, and meet potential spouses. Parents who say "finish your degree, then think about marriage" have created a false sequence. Wise parents pursue both tracks at once—building durable agency while actively facilitating the relationships that lead to marriage.

OBJECTION: "RIGOROUS FORMATION REPLACES TRUST IN GOD"

This concern is the most serious. If we form daughters to have durable agency "in case" marriage fails or a husband dies, are we not hedging against providence rather than trusting it?

The concern assumes that rigorous formation and faith in God are mutually exclusive—that preparing practically somehow diminishes trusting spiritually. But these are independent dimensions. Rigorous formation is the active process of building capacity. Faith is the belief that God is sovereign over all things. One needs both.

Rigor without faith leads to secular living—treating demanding training as the end when it is only the means. The daughter formed this way builds capacity but orients it toward her own security rather than God's purposes. Faith without rigor is passivity disguised as trust—and in its extreme, produces nothing. It is the servant in the Parable of the Talents who buried what he was given rather than putting it to work (Matthew 25:24–30). The master did not commend his "trust."

He condemned his failure to act.

But the deeper error in this objection is the premise itself. The primary reason for rigorous formation is not "in case something goes wrong." The primary reason is that biblical womanhood requires it.

Biblical womanhood is not passive. It requires capability, discernment, and strength under authority. A daughter without durable agency is not positioned for biblical submission—she is positioned for dependence confused with submission. Rigorous formation serves the expected case, not merely the contingencies. The benefits of being prepared if circumstances change are real but secondary.

9

THE CHILD'S POSTURE

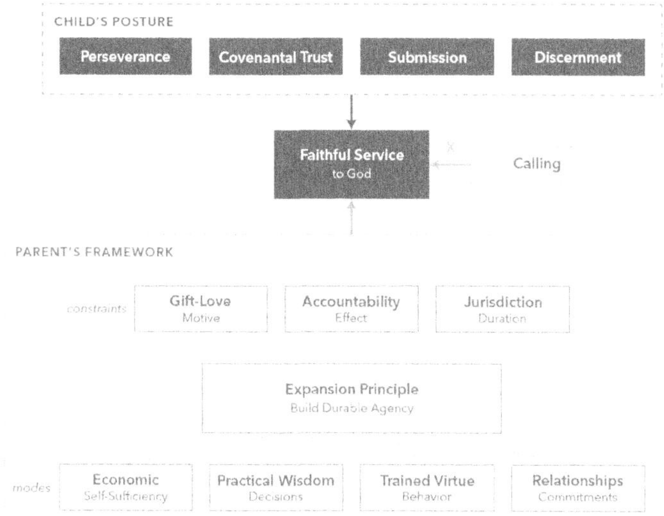

Up to this point, the framework has addressed what parents do. How a child engages formation matters as much as how a parent directs it. That engagement requires four capacities: perseverance, submission, covenantal trust, and discernment.

DOMAIN	PARENT SIDE	CHILD SIDE
Goal	Expansion Principle	Perseverance
Motive	Gift-Love Constraint	Covenantal Trust
Limits	Accountability Constraint	Discernment
Authority	Jurisdiction Constraint	Submission

Perseverance is the capacity to continue when the task is hard—to sustain effort through difficulty without quitting when discomfort arrives. Chapter 7 described how this capacity is built early through structured activities, age-appropriate work, and the experience of pushing through the repetitions that actually build strength. A child who lacks perseverance cannot sustain demanding vocational formation regardless of the path chosen.

Submission is the capacity to move forward under direction one did not choose—to accept parental authority even when preferences conflict. Chapter 7 described how this capacity is built through years of practice on small things. True submission reveals itself precisely when one disagrees—agreement is not submission; it is merely doing what one already wanted.

The remainder of this chapter addresses the other two: covenantal trust and discernment.

Consider a nineteen-year-old son whose parents are directing him toward an electrical apprenticeship. He likes electrical work—he is good with his hands, enjoys solving wiring problems, and finds the logic of circuits satisfying. But he likes pharmacy studies more. He has always been drawn to science, did well in chemistry, and pictures himself behind a counter helping patients understand their medications. He wants to pursue a Doctor of Pharmacy degree.

His parents see the math differently. The apprenticeship costs nothing—he earns while he learns. Within four years he would be a licensed journeyman electrician earning strong wages with zero debt, in a trade that cannot be outsourced or automated. Pharmacy school requires at least four years of education, and graduates carry $150,000 or more in student debt. The pharmacy job market has tightened in recent years. His parents are not wealthy. They cannot fund this path, and they believe the debt would limit his ability to give generously, support a family, and serve freely for years, possibly a decade.

Both sides have reasonable arguments. The son is not being foolish. The parents are not acting from need-love. Many parents in this situation would let the child decide and that would be entirely reasonable. But these parents believe the financial risk is too high for their family, and they have made the call. The framework permits both approaches. What matters here is not which decision is correct but how the son responds to direction he did not choose.

What happens next reveals posture, not preference. The son who practices submission says: "I think pharmacy is the better path, and here is why. But I hear your reasoning, and I'll move forward with the apprenticeship. I want you to know I disagree—and I want to keep talking about this as I prove myself." He stays engaged. He voices his perspective. He moves forward under direction he did not choose. He does not like the decision. But he knows that the relationship with his parents matters more than which career he enters at nineteen.

The son who capitulates says nothing. He enrolls in the

apprenticeship and does fine—because he actually likes the work. But something has shifted. Conversations become superficial. Visits stay pleasant but short. He does not fight. He does not argue. There is no crisis. He simply stops sharing his life with his parents—not because he dislikes the path, but because they did not let him choose it. The career worked. The relationship became shallow. Two years later, his parents believe the decision went well. Their son would say the closeness is gone.

The difference between these two outcomes has almost nothing to do with the career decision. It has everything to do with whether the son learned, long before this moment arrived, that what he wants and what he does are not always the same thing and that staying connected to the people he disagrees with is more important than winning the argument or letting resentment quietly replace relationship.

CONTRACT VS. COVENANTAL TRUST

A contract is an exchange: I give you this, you give me that. If one side fails to deliver, the other side can walk away. The relationship lasts only as long as both sides hold up their end. Contractual thinking in a family sounds like this: "If my parents do not act from pure gift-love, I do not have to obey." The child becomes the judge of parental motive—and can exit whenever the verdict falls short. But submission to imperfect authority requires something deeper: a kind of trust that does not depend on parental perfection.

Consider how God related to Israel. His people worshiped golden calves, chased false gods, ignored prophets, and broke every promise they made. By contractual logic, God should have walked away. He did not. He pursued, disciplined, restored, and stayed faithful—not because Israel earned it, but because He had bound Himself to them.

The child's relationship with parents is not the same as God's covenant with Israel. But the posture of trust should look similar. Scripture consistently presents faithful relationships—God to Israel, Christ to the church, husband to wife—as marked by commitment that outlasts failure. The child's trust in parents need not rise to the level of a formal covenant to reflect this pattern; however, a child who withholds trust until parents prove their motives are pure has adopted contractual thinking. A child who extends trust despite imperfect parental judgment reflects how God relates to His people.

Most teaching on children's obedience rests on two ideas: God commands it, or parents know better. But both can fall short when a child truly believes the parent is wrong about their future. "Because God says so" feels empty when the real question is about career direction. "Because we know better" is exactly what the child disputes. There is a third basis—and it runs deeper than either.

Does the child believe that God is sovereign over all things? If so, then God gave this child these particular parents with these particular limitations. The same God who shapes the child's future also chose the family in which that shaping would occur. A child cannot trust God's sovereignty selectively—embracing it when circumstances feel favorable and rejecting it when parents disappoint. Covenantal trust means believing that God, in His providence, works through imperfect parents just as He works through imperfect churches, imperfect pastors, and imperfect circumstances.

This does not mean trust without limits. The Discernment section addresses when parental direction crosses into genuine harm. But ordinary imperfection—even significant error in judgment—does not release the child from a covenantal posture. Parents will sometimes be wrong. They may even be partially corrupted by need-love. Covenantal trust does not require believing that parents are right. It requires believing that they love you—and trusting that God can accomplish His purposes through their direction even when that direction proves to be mistaken. Consider a daughter who wanted art school but whose parents directed her toward nursing. She advocated her perspective, heard them hold firm, and completed the degree without bitterness—not because she stopped believing art was a better fit, but because she trusted that God could work through her parents' imperfect judgment.

DISCERNMENT

Covenantal trust is not blind trust. It operates alongside a fourth capacity: discernment. Discernment is the capacity to recognize when difficulty has crossed into destruction or when authority has crossed into abuse. It is the child-side mirror of the Accountability Constraint: the parent monitors for breakdown from the outside; the child recognizes it from the inside. This capacity develops later than perseverance and submission because it requires the maturity to distinguish "I dislike this" from "this is harming me."

A child must first discern whether this is ordinary disagreement or systemic breakdown. Children naturally resist difficult paths. Before seeking external counsel, a child should examine their own heart: Am I resisting because this path threatens genuine harm, or because it conflicts with my preferences? This discernment should be grounded in gospel truth because their identity is secured in Christ, not in vocational outcomes or parental approval. That security is what allows honest self-examination.

In cases of ordinary disagreement, the child should first remember what they share with their parents and enjoy being in their presence before tackling the differences that divide them. From that foundation they can pursue reconciliation: understand parental reasoning, seek common ground, and cultivate multiple accountability structures—church, mentors, friends, and professionals. Children should recognize that everyone has biases: they may gravitate toward counsel that validates their preferences, church leaders may reflexively defer to parental authority, and parents may be blind to their own need-love. The goal is a restored relationship, not a maximized outcome.

When the concern is systemic breakdown—persistent inability despite sincere effort, escalating psychological crisis, or patterns of deterioration—the situation is fundamentally different. The first priority is assessment, not relationship restoration. Subjective distress alone does not constitute systemic breakdown; evidence requires confirmation from multiple sources—professional assessment, documented symptoms over time, and decline in functioning across multiple domains. The child's next step is outside counsel—not unilateral action. This means seeking input from church elders and pastors, mature Christian adults outside the immediate family, professionals who can provide objective assessment, or trusted mentors who can offer external accountability. Disobeying authority God has established is a grave decision that should rarely occur and never without such counsel.

Seeking church counsel is not disobedience but an act within the structure of obedience. The child who appeals to elders submits the question to legitimate authority rather than making autonomous judgment. The elders adjudicate; the child does not self-authorize. This preserves the Fifth Commandment: the child honors parents by seeking external discernment rather than either silent compliance with destruction or unilateral rebellion.

But the goal is adjudication, not validation. A child who approaches elders hoping they will overrule unwanted parental direction has misunderstood the process. The church's role is to discern whether parents have violated the framework's constraints, not whether the child dislikes the path. Practically, this means that the child should come prepared with facts: What has the parent directed? What evidence suggests harm rather than productive difficulty? How long has the pattern persisted? Elders cannot adjudicate well without concrete information. The child should also expect elders to contact the parents—church accountability is not conducted behind parental backs.

In an ideal scenario, the child must be prepared to accept the elders' judgment—even if it supports the parents. Submitting the question to the church means accepting the church's discernment, not appealing until someone agrees with you.

However, we live in a fallen world. Every church believes it is functional; every member who attends believes the same. I do not doubt the good intentions of most churches. But church leadership may be corrupt, complicit, or incompetent. They may default to parental authority or act on incomplete information. In such cases, the framework's safeguards are harder to operationalize. This is a limitation of applying any Christian ethical framework in a fallen world, not a failure of the framework itself. As such, it is imperative that a child seeks counsel from diverse sources—both within and outside the church, from people with varied backgrounds and perspectives.

Children in isolated families—where parents have cut off counselors, left churches, or dismissed concerned relatives—face a harder path. The ordinary channels of accountability have been closed. In such cases, mandatory reporters become essential: teachers, doctors, and school counselors who are legally required to act when they suspect harm. A child in this situation is not betraying their family by speaking to such adults. They are seeking the protection their parents have refused to provide.

GENUINE ABUSE

In cases of genuine abuse—whether physical violence, patterns of severe emotional manipulation, or spiritual coercion that weaponizes God's authority to control or harm—the framework changes entirely. Abuse requires immediate protection, not gradual discernment through the ordinary pathways.

Children experiencing abuse should seek immediate safety through trusted adults, civil authorities, or protective services as the situation requires. Separation may be necessary and appropriate—not as punishment but as protection for both child and parent.

God's command to honor parents does not require children to enable their own destruction. Seeking protection is not rebellion but responsible stewardship of the life God has given. The obligation to honor parents in such cases is fulfilled through seeking help that protects the child and creates accountability that might lead to parental repentance and restoration—though safety, not reconciliation, is the immediate priority. Some abusive parents never repent, and children are not morally responsible for that outcome.

THE DEFAULT POSTURE

Children cannot demand that parents act from purely Christ-like motivations before obeying. Parents are fallen beings who will sin, just as children are fallen and may pursue their own preferences while claiming godly motives. The default posture must be obedient trust in God's sovereignty over the formation He has ordained, with the church, not the individual child, serving as the proper check when parental authority becomes destructive.

The child who develops all four capacities—perseverance through difficulty, covenantal trust toward fallible parents, submission to authority, and discernment to recognize when lines have been crossed—possesses the complete toolkit for navigating formation. These capacities do not ensure easy passage. They equip the child to engage formation rightly: enduring what should be endured, accepting what should be accepted, trusting what should be trusted, and appealing when appeal is warranted.

10

CONCLUSION

Do parents have the authority to direct—or even demand—that their child follow a specific vocational path? The structure I have outlined suggests the answer is not a simple yes or no. It depends on the 1+3 framework this book has developed: one governing principle (expansion of durable agency) bounded by three constraints (gift-love, accountability, jurisdiction). Demanding vocational formation can legitimately build the competence, resources, and options that create future independence, including the option to eventually change direction.

But parents act under uncertainty. They cannot know in advance whether their judgment is correct for their particular child. The framework provides authority to direct formation, but it also creates an obligation: to watch for evidence of misjudgment and adjust when it accumulates. That uncertainty is precisely why parents need criteria beyond "it worked for me" or "I turned out okay." Personal outcomes, good or bad, do not establish principles.

WHAT THE FRAMEWORK CANNOT DO

This framework cannot guarantee outcomes. A child formed with wisdom and love may still drift. A child formed poorly may still flourish by God's grace. And some children will reject everything their parents built, not because formation failed, but because the child chose a different path. The grief of watching this happen does not always go away. But even here, the gospel holds. The same Savior who pursued a rebellious Israel pursues rebellious children, and the parent's faithfulness in formation is not measured by the child's response to it. Formation is not a formula that produces predetermined results. It is faithful stewardship of the authority God has given, exercised under uncertainty, accountable to Him for the process even when the outcome remains beyond parental control.

The framework also does not answer every question. A framework that attempted to answer every application question would fail the diversity of real families. The immigrant family stretching to fund one child's education faces different tradeoffs than the family with resources for all. The son with chronic illness requires different calibration than his healthy sister. The church community in a developing country operates with different assumptions about marriage timing than one living in suburban America. Prescriptive specificity would produce a framework that works for some families while failing others.

Nor can the framework do what only God can do: produce a living faith in your child. Durable agency without faith is capacity without direction. This book addresses how to build it. It assumes that parents will also faithfully expose their children to Scripture, prayer, worship, and Christian community—the ordinary means through which God works to kindle faith. But faith itself is His gift, not their achievement.

No framework eliminates uncertainty. Parents will still make mistakes, misjudge their children, and fall short of their own intentions. But they need not act blindly. They can direct toward durable agency, examine their motives, adjust when there is evidence of systemic breakdown, and release authority when the season ends. The rest is faithfulness.

WHAT FAITHFUL FORMATION PRODUCES

Remember the thirty-two-year-old from Chapter 1—living in a studio apartment, on his fourth career pivot, undirected. Remember the twenty-seven-year-old in marketing, making a decent living but unprepared for what happens when life applies real pressure. Their parents loved them. Their parents also made formation decisions, whether by action or inaction, that contributed to where they landed.

Now imagine a different outcome. A thirty-two-year-old who can support a household, who weathered job loss without crisis, who has the practical wisdom to navigate complex decisions and the character to be trusted with responsibility. A twenty-seven-year-old who works hard but has margin—financial stability, relational depth, the capacity to weather whatever comes rather than be undone by it. These adults are not guaranteed happiness. They face the same fallen world as everyone else. But they face it with durable agency—the sustained capacity to direct their own lives in faithful service to God.

This is what formation aims to produce: not perfect children, but capable adults. Adults who can establish households, raise the next generation, serve the church, and steward whatever calling God reveals precisely because their parents built the platform from which such service becomes possible.

Parents reading this book face a choice. Not whether to shape their children—that will happen regardless. The choice is whether to shape them with intention or by default, with criteria or by intuition, with accountability or in isolation.

The framework I have offered does not make formation easy. It makes formation *structured*. It gives parents language for decisions they already face, criteria for evaluating paths they already consider, and guardrails for authority they already possess. Parents who disagree about whether engineering or nursing better builds durable agency for their particular child are having the right argument—an argument the framework structures without resolving.

THE STAKES

The stakes are not merely economic. They are generational. Parents who form well produce adults who can form the next generation well. Parents who drift produce adults who lack the capacity to do otherwise. The patterns compound. A family that builds durable agency across generations creates an inheritance far more valuable than money—a legacy of capability, wisdom, and faithfulness that equips each generation to serve God from a position of strength rather than scrambling from a position of weakness.

This is why formation cannot be left to intuition, cultural defaults, or the hope that children will "figure it out." The gray zone is real. The choices matter. And parents who take formation seriously—who direct with gift-love, watch for breakdown, and release authority when the season ends—are not only giving a gift to their children, but also to their children's children and the generations that follow.

May we form wisely, watch carefully, and love deeply. And where we fall short, may God's grace cover both us and our children.

APPENDIX A

FRAMEWORK DIAGRAM

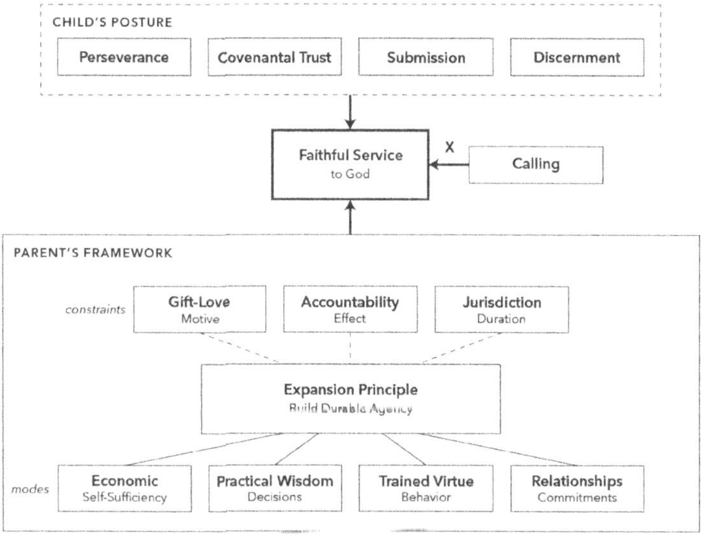

APPENDIX B

LOGIC CHAIN

P1: Parents have divinely ordained authority over children

P2: Parental authority is a temporary stewardship

P3: The ultimate purpose of formation is spiritual: children capable of knowing and faithfully serving God across a lifetime

P4: But parents cannot directly produce spiritual outcomes; faith is God's gift through the Spirit

P5: Therefore, parents need a knowable, operational criterion to guide formation decisions

P6: The natural candidate is calling

P7: But calling cannot be reliably discerned before formation

P8: Calling may become intelligible retrospectively, but this arrives too late to guide formation decisions

P9: Therefore, parents need a criterion that is concrete, observable, and serves the spiritual purpose

P10: That criterion is durable agency—the sustained capacity to direct one's own life, enabling lifelong faithful service to God

P11: Durable agency is built through modes which include: economic self-sufficiency, practical wisdom, trained virtue, and relational capacity

P12: Each mode includes a spiritual dimension that orients it toward ultimate purpose

P13: Formation is legitimate when it expands durable agency through these modes (Expansion Principle)

P14: But formation must be motivated by gift-love, not need-love (Gift-Love Constraint)

P15: Formation must be adjusted when systemic breakdown occurs (Accountability Constraint)

P16: Parental directive authority must terminate upon marriage (Jurisdiction Constraint)

P17: These constraints apply equally to sons and daughters

P18: Children's obligation to obey operates within these same constraints

C1: Therefore, parental authority to direct formation is legitimate but bounded by motive (gift-love), consequences (accountability), and duration (jurisdiction).

C2: Formation succeeds when durable agency is built, producing adults capable of knowing and faithfully serving God across a lifetime.

A NOTE ON STRUCTURE: The logic chain establishes that parental authority is bounded by knowable criteria serving an ultimate spiritual purpose; the book's structure explains *why* Christians should embrace these bounds and how to apply them faithfully.

APPENDIX C

GLOSSARY OF KEY TERMS

ACCOUNTABILITY CONSTRAINT—Parents must respond to evidence of systemic breakdown by adjusting formation. Parents need not prove in advance that their direction will work, but they must adjust when evidence accumulates that they misjudged.

COVENANTAL TRUST—The child's posture of trust toward imperfect parents, grounded in God's sovereignty over the family He ordained. Unlike contractual thinking, it extends commitment despite imperfect parental judgment.

DISCERNMENT—The child-side capacity to recognize when difficulty has crossed into destruction or authority has crossed into abuse. It mirrors the Accountability Constraint for parents.

DURABLE AGENCY—The sustained capacity to direct one's own life. It is built through modes and replaces calling as the knowable criterion for formation decisions.

EXPANSION PRINCIPLE—The framework's governing

principle: formation is legitimate when it expands durable agency.

GIFT-LOVE—The desire to give, serve, and sacrifice for a child's good with no strings attached. Drawn from C. S. Lewis's *The Four Loves*, it is distinguished from need-love.

GIFT-LOVE CONSTRAINT—Formation must be motivated by the child's good, not the parent's need for validation. A good outcome does not justify a bad motive.

GRAY ZONE, THE—The distinctly modern period (roughly ages eighteen to thirty) created by infinite vocational choice, delayed marriage, and extended education, where children lack clear direction but have not yet established independent households.

JURISDICTION CONSTRAINT—Parental directive authority is time-bounded, extending until marriage in most cases. Parents have an obligation to actively facilitate marriage, not merely wait passively or veto prospects indefinitely.

MODES OF DURABLE AGENCY—Observable capacity formation develops including: economic self-sufficiency, practical wisdom, trained virtue, and relational capacity. These modes work together, and each has a spiritual dimension.

NEED-LOVE—The parent's longing to be needed, to feel secure, or to have a child's outcomes prove something about the parent's worth. It can drive both controlling and permissive parenting.

1+3 FRAMEWORK, THE—The framework's structure: one governing principle (Expansion) bounded by three constraints addressing motive (Gift-Love), consequences (Accountability), and duration (Jurisdiction).

PERSEVERANCE—The capacity to sustain effort through difficulty without quitting. It is distinct from submission: a child may persist through chosen difficulty yet refuse to accept direction when preferences conflict.

PRODUCTIVE STRUGGLE—Difficulty that builds capacity. It typically shows improvement over time and stays contained in the demanding area.

SUBMISSION—Obeying while staying relationally engaged—the child shares disagreement, then moves forward under direction. It is distinguished from capitulation (obeying while withdrawing), rebellion (refusing while engaged), and passive resistance (refusing while withdrawn).

SYSTEMIC BREAKDOWN—Persistent patterns of failure, crisis, or deterioration signaling that formation is destroying capacity rather than building it. One difficult semester is not breakdown; three years of declining function is.

REFERENCES

1. Lewis, C. S. *The Four Loves*. Harcourt, Brace, 1960.
2. Erikson, E. H. *Identity: Youth and Crisis*. W. W. Norton & Company, 1968.
3. Leu, Katrina. *Beginning College Students Who Change Their Majors Within 3 Years of Enrollment*. NCES 2018-434. National Center for Education Statistics, U.S. Department of Education, 2017. https://nces.ed.gov/pubs2018/2018434.pdf.
4. MacIntyre, Alasdair. *After Virtue: A Study in Moral Theory*. 3rd ed. University of Notre Dame Press, 2007.
5. Aristotle. *Nicomachean Ethics*. Translated by W. D. Ross. In *The Basic Works of Aristotle*, edited by R. McKeon. Random House, 1941.
6. Aquinas, Thomas. *Summa Theologica*. Translated by Fathers of the English Dominican Province. Benziger Bros., 1947.

7. History, Art & Archives, U.S. House of Representatives. "The Twenty-sixth Amendment." https://history.house.gov/Historical-Highlights/1951-2000/The-26th-Amendment/.

8. Council of Europe, Committee of Ministers. Resolution (72) 29 on the Lowering of the Age of Full Legal Capacity. Adopted September 19, 1972. Council of Europe, 1973.

9. United Nations. Convention on the Rights of the Child. November 20, 1989. United Nations Treaty Series, vol. 1577, p. 3.

10. Baumrind, Diana. "The Influence of Parenting Style on Adolescent Competence and Substance Use." *The Journal of Early Adolescence* 11, no. 1 (1991): 56–95. https://doi.org/10.1177/0272431691111004.

11. Pinquart, Martin. "Associations of Parenting Dimensions and Styles with Academic Achievement in Children and Adolescents: A Meta-Analysis." *Educational Psychology Review* 28, no. 3 (2016): 475–93. https://doi.org/10.1007/s10648-015-9338-y.

12. Pinquart, Martin. "Associations of Parenting Dimensions and Styles with Externalizing Problems of Children and Adolescents: An Updated Meta-Analysis." *Developmental Psychology* 53, no. 5 (2017): 873–932. https://doi.org/10.1037/dev0000295.

13. Singh-Manoux, Archana, Peter Fonagy, and Michael Marmot. "The Relationship Between Parenting Dimensions and Adult Achievement: Evidence from the Whitehall II Study." *International Journal of Behavioral Medicine* 13, no. 4 (2006): 320–29. https://doi.org/10.1207/s15327558ijbm1304_7.

14. Calvin, John. *Commentary on the Epistles of Paul the Apostle to the Corinthians.* In *Calvin's Commentaries,* vol. 20. Translated by John Pringle. Baker, 1996.

PART II

CASE STUDIES

INTRODUCTION

The framework is now complete. What remains is to test it. No framework, however carefully reasoned, captures every situation. The world is too complex, families too varied, children too particular. This framework does not pretend otherwise. It provides criteria for thinking—not prescriptions for deciding. Parents who share its commitments may examine the same child and reach opposite conclusions. That is not failure; it is the nature of exercising judgment under uncertainty.

What follows are five case studies designed to surface common tensions—extreme by design, because sharper contrasts make the principles more visible. Each presents a scenario where the principles pull in different directions, where reasonable applications conflict, where the 'right answer' depends on facts and judgments that only the family involved can fully assess.

Each case follows a consistent structure: the scenario, reflection questions for parents, reflection questions for the child, and questions for both to consider together. The goal is not to be prescriptive, but to ensure the right questions are being asked and discussed.

CASE STUDY #1 (Sam: High Durable Agency vs. Passion Path)

CASE STUDY #2 (Emma: The Cost of Deferral)

CASE STUDY #3 (Claire: Success but Destroyed Relationship)

CASE STUDY #4 (David: Agency Without Faith)

CASE STUDY #5 (Ethan: Missions vs. Durable Agency)

CASE STUDY #1

HIGH DURABLE AGENCY VS. PASSION PATH

Does the Expansion Principle require maximizing durable agency even when it means forcing mediocrity, or does exceptional competence in a lower-agency path satisfy the principle? Must parents always choose the highest-agency path available, or can exceptional ability in a different field justify a different direction?

Sam is seventeen, a high school senior facing a pivotal decision: engineering school or art school. His parents insist on engineering. Sam desperately wants art. Both sides have compelling arguments.

SAM'S ARTISTIC PROFILE

Sam has exceptional artistic talent. At fourteen, he won a national young artists competition. At fifteen, his work was exhibited in a regional gallery. At sixteen, he completed a summer intensive at a prestigious art institute where his instructor—a working artist with gallery representation in New York—told his parents:

"Your son has something rare. I see hundreds of talented students. Sam has both technical mastery and genuine artistic vision. If he commits to serious training, he could have a significant career."

The professional art instructor has offered specific guidance: "Four-year Bachelor of Fine Arts from strong program, followed by two-year Master of Fine Arts (MFA). During college: summer residencies, build portfolio, start submitting to juried shows. After MFA: adjunct teaching for income stability while building gallery presence. This is the pathway for serious artists. It's not a guarantee, but Sam has the talent to make it viable."

SAM'S ACADEMIC PROFILE

His academic record in STEM is different. He's competent but not exceptional: B+ average in AP Calculus and Physics, solid but unspectacular SAT math scores (680), adequate performance in chemistry but no particular affinity. His teachers describe him as "capable but not passionate" in technical subjects. He works hard enough to keep up but shows no intrinsic interest. He forgets formulas between exams, struggles with three-dimensional visualization in physics, and finds lab work tedious.

PARENTS' PERSPECTIVE

His parents are immigrants. His father is a civil engineer who worked his way from drafting technician to project manager through evening classes and certifications. His mother is a hospital administrator who started as a nursing assistant. They built a stable middle-class life through technical credentials and steady employment.

They watched cousins and neighbors struggle—the

charismatic restaurant manager who lost everything in the 2008 recession, the talented musician working three part-time jobs in his forties, the graphic designer whose freelance income disappeared during the COVID pandemic. From their perspective: engineering is the path to stability. Engineers earn stable above-average income, have clear career progression, weather recessions better than most professions, and can support families reliably.

They've told Sam: "We will pay for engineering school. We will not pay for art school. If you want art, you can pursue it after you have an engineering degree and a stable job. You can take art classes as electives. You can paint on weekends. But you will not risk your future on something so uncertain."

His parents counter with data: median income for fine artists is $50k, many earn far less, adjunct teaching pays $3k–$5k per course with no benefits or job security, more than half of art school graduates are underemployed relative to their education level, and the "successful artist" often depends on family wealth to subsidize the lean years. Even the instructor admits: "I teach to pay bills and make art on the side. That's reality for most of us."

SAM'S PERSPECTIVE

Sam argues back: "I'll be a mediocre engineer at best. I have real talent in art. Shouldn't I pursue what I could actually excel at rather than what I'll just be okay at? You're asking me to trade excellence for security."

THE DECISION POINT

Sam is now seventeen, with acceptance letters from both the state flagship school ($30k/year) and an elite art school ($60k/

year). His parents have made it clear: they will pay for an engineering education but not for the art school. If he wants art school, he can take loans, but they won't co-sign. The financial structure makes engineering the only viable path unless he's willing to graduate with $240k in debt for an art degree.

REFLECTION QUESTIONS FOR PARENTS

EXPANSION PRINCIPLE

- The Expansion Principle says formation is legitimate when it expands durable agency. Sam's parents see a clear winner: engineering builds more agency than art. But Sam argues he would be mediocre at engineering and exceptional at art. Does the principle measure the path's potential—or the child's potential on that path? Is mediocre agency on a high-ceiling track better than exceptional agency on a lower one?

- If Sam pursues engineering and succeeds, he gains economic stability but may serve God from a place of quiet resentment. If he pursues art and succeeds, he may serve with deep conviction but limited means. Which outcome better positions him for faithful service across a lifetime—and which gap is easier to close later?

GIFT-LOVE CONSTRAINT

- Why do I specifically want Sam to go into engineering? If Sam wanted nursing or accounting instead, how would I respond? What does my answer reveal about whether my concern is truly about his capacity for faithful service or is something else driving my insistence on this specific engineering path?

- Need-love often hides beneath gift-love. When I imagine Sam succeeding as an artist—building a life I did not pursue—what feelings surface? What might those feelings reveal about whose good I am protecting?

- The framework argues that parents can only sustain gift-love when their worth isn't tied to their child's outcomes. If Sam pursues engineering and resents us, or pursues art and struggles—can we hold either outcome without our identity collapsing? What would it look like to direct him firmly while genuinely believing that Christ's finished work, not Sam's success, determines our standing before God?

ACCOUNTABILITY CONSTRAINT

- Sam is competent but mediocre in engineering—B+ grades, no intrinsic interest. The framework says competence can generate meaning over time. But the framework also says the Accountability Constraint requires adjustment when formation causes systematic breakdown. How do we tell the difference between a child who hasn't yet discovered meaning in a difficult path and a child who is slowly breaking under one? What would we need to see—and how long would we need to see it—before we could answer that question with confidence?

- The Accountability Constraint requires adjustment when formation causes harm. But adjustment is harder when I have already invested in particular direction. If two years into engineering, Sam is failing despite real effort, withdrawing from relationships, or showing signs of serious distress—how will I adjust? Can I picture myself saying "I was wrong about this path for you"?

- The Accountability Constraint depends on information—I cannot adjust to what I cannot see. Sam will only share his struggles if he believes honesty is safe. When he has brought me hard news in the past, how have I responded? Did my reaction make him more likely to come to me next time, or less?

- How does pushing him into engineering change the relationship? Five years from now, if he has the degree but we barely speak, will the formation have succeeded or failed? What does my answer reveal about what I am actually trying to build?

JURISDICTION CONSTRAINT

- Sam is seventeen—still within the formation window, but approaching adulthood. When he was twelve, he needed to obey; his capacity for reasoning about his future was limited. At seventeen, he brings reasoned arguments, demonstrated ability, and a clearer sense of his strengths. How should his growing maturity shape how I exercise authority now? Can I explain my reasoning in terms he would recognize as genuine concern for his good? When I speak to him about this decision, does he hear a parent preparing him for independence, or a parent who will not be questioned?

REFLECTION QUESTIONS FOR CHILD

EXAMINING SELF

- Am I pursuing art because I genuinely believe it's the path toward faithful service to God, or because it's what I want right now and I'm using spiritual language to justify preference? Am I resisting because I genuinely cannot sustain this path, or because it is hard and I do not enjoy it right now?

- I resist engineering because I believe I would be mediocre at it and find it joyless. But the framework claims that competence can generate meaning over time. If engineering turned out to be more engaging than I expect, would I be open to discovering that? Or have I already decided I will hate it—making the outcome certain before the experiment begins?

UNDERSTANDING PARENTS

- My parents immigrated with little and built stability through years of demanding work. The life I have grown up in—the house, the education, the options I now take for granted—came from their sacrifice. When they talk about economic security, what are they remembering? What did it cost them to build what I have inherited?

- I am seventeen. I have not yet paid rent, supported a family, or weathered a recession. My parents have done all of these things. They have watched talented people struggle and seen stable careers provide options that artistic ones did not. What might they see about adult life—about what it actually takes to sustain a household over decades—that I cannot yet see from where I stand?

SUBMISSION AND TRUST

- The framework describes four possible responses to unwanted direction: rebellion, passive resistance, capitulation, and submission. Which am I choosing? Which am I capable of choosing?

- The framework rests on a claim about God's sovereignty—that He works through imperfect parents just as He works through imperfect churches and imperfect circumstances. If my parents direct me toward engineering and they turn out to be wrong, can I trust that God might still accomplish His purposes through their flawed judgment? What would it look like to walk a path I did not choose—honoring my parents without pretending I agree—while genuinely believing God is present in it?

- The framework distinguishes covenantal trust from contractual trust. Contractual thinking says: "If my parents don't act from pure gift-love, I don't have to obey." Covenantal trust extends trust despite imperfect parental judgment—believing they are *for* me even when I think they're wrong. Which posture am I adopting? What would it cost me to trust that God can work through my parents' flawed direction?

QUESTIONS FOR BOTH

- Disagreements can be conducted in ways that preserve relationship or ways that poison it. When we argue about this decision, what happens between us? Do we leave conversations feeling heard—even when we still disagree—or do we leave feeling dismissed, controlled, or wounded?

- We each believe we're right—and we each have reasons. But one of us has decades of experience the other lacks, and the other has self-knowledge the first may be dismissing. Whose judgment should carry more weight in this decision—and on what basis? Where does parental authority end and the child's ownership of their own life begin when the child is seventeen and the stakes are permanent?

- If Sam submits and pursues engineering, what does he need from us to make that path survivable—not just academically, but relationally and spiritually? If we adjust and support art, what do we need from Sam to trust that he is taking the economic risks seriously and not just choosing the path of least resistance?

- Five years from now, Sam will be twenty-two. What outcome would we both look back on with gratitude—not just "it worked out," but "we handled this well"? What would we need to do now to make that future possible?

CASE STUDY #2

THE COST OF DEFERRAL

What happens when parents decline to direct—when they defer to preference, avoid conflict, and trust their child to find their own way? If the framework requires active formation, what does formation's absence produce?

Emma is thirty-five, living in her childhood bedroom. She works at a coffee shop near her parents' house, earning $18 an hour plus tips. Fourteen years after graduating, she is in the same role she took as a "temporary" job while figuring things out. She has a bachelor's degree in philosophy from a good state university.

Emma is not lazy. She reads widely, thinks deeply, and can hold her own in any conversation. Her managers consistently praise her work ethic and her way with customers. She has been promoted twice—first to shift supervisor, then to assistant manager—but turned down both promotions because they felt like "settling into something I never chose."

Her parents, Michael and Jennifer, are successful professionals. Michael is an orthopedic surgeon. Jennifer is a corporate attorney who made partner at thirty-eight. They met at Stanford, married at twenty-six, and built a life of stability and achievement. They raised Emma with every advantage: good schools, travel, books, exposure to ideas. They also raised her with a philosophy: children should discover their own path.

THE PHILOSOPHY

Michael and Jennifer did not arrive at their parenting approach carelessly. They thought about it. They read books. They discussed it with friends who shared their values. They were reacting against their own upbringings—Michael's father had demanded he become a doctor, and though Michael eventually loved medicine, he remembered the pressure as suffocating. Jennifer's mother had mapped out her entire career before she finished high school, leaving Jennifer feeling like she was living someone else's life until her thirties.

They decided their daughter would have what they lacked: freedom to become herself. They would provide resources, encouragement, and unconditional support. They would not impose their expectations. They would trust Emma to find her way.

When fourteen-year-old Emma wanted to drop competitive swimming—where she was genuinely talented—because practices were "too early and too hard," they let her. "She knows what's right for her," Jennifer told Michael. "Forcing her to continue would just make her resent it." When sixteen-year-old Emma wanted to take art classes instead of AP Chemistry, they supported her. "She's not going to be a scientist," Michael reasoned. "Why make her miserable in a class she'll never use?"

When seventeen-year-old Emma couldn't decide between several colleges, they told her to "go with her gut." She chose the school where she'd felt happiest during the campus visit—a reasonable state university with a strong philosophy department and a beautiful campus. She had been accepted to more rigorous schools, but those visits felt "too intense."

When twenty-one-year-old Emma graduated with a philosophy degree and no job prospects, they told her to "take time to figure things out." She moved home "temporarily." The temporary stay is now entering its fourteenth year.

THE DRIFT

Emma's twenties have been a series of starts without finishes. After graduation, she worked at a bookstore while "exploring options." She considered law school but decided the LSAT felt too much like "jumping through hoops." She looked into graduate programs in philosophy but concluded that academia was "too narrow." She took an interest in user experience design, completed an online certificate, then decided the field was "too corporate." She trained as a yoga instructor, taught for eight months, then stopped because the studio's approach felt "inauthentic."

Each pivot made sense at the time. Each decision to stop felt like self-knowledge—learning what didn't fit. But the pattern accumulated. At thirty-five, Emma has explored many things and built nothing. She has no career trajectory, no savings, no clear path toward the independent life her parents assumed would naturally emerge.

She is also single, though this bothers her parents more than it bothers her. She has dated occasionally but describes relationships as "distracting from figuring myself out." Her social life centers on a small group of friends from college—most of whom are also underemployed, also living with or near parents, also still "figuring things out."

THE PARENTS NOW

Michael and Jennifer are sixty-two and sixty. They had planned to retire at sixty-five, travel, enjoy grandchildren. Those plans are on hold. Emma still needs support—not dramatic support, but steady support. She pays no rent. Her car is on their insurance. Her health coverage is through Michael's plan. Her student loans, which her parents co-signed, are being paid at the minimum rate because Emma cannot afford more.

More than the money, they feel a creeping grief they cannot name. Their daughter—bright, capable, raised with every advantage—is stuck. And they do not understand what went wrong.

Michael, in a rare moment of honesty with his brother: "We gave her everything. Freedom. Support. We never pressured her. We trusted her. And now she's thirty-five, still in the same job she took right after college. What did we do wrong?"

Jennifer, to her therapist: "I keep wondering if we should have pushed harder. But that felt so wrong at the time. We didn't want to be our parents. We wanted Emma to be herself. Now I look at her, and I don't know who she is. I don't think she knows either."

EMMA'S PERSPECTIVE

Emma does not see herself as a failure. She sees herself as someone who refused to settle for a life she didn't choose. She rejected paths that felt wrong. She honored her instincts. She stayed true to herself.

But lately, something has shifted. Friends from college are getting married, buying houses, having children. Her social media feed is full of people her age living lives that look like adult lives. She tells herself she doesn't want those things—but she's less sure than she used to be.

She told her therapist: "My parents always said I could be anything. But I don't know how to be anything. I know how to think about what I want. I don't know how to build something. Every time I start something, I see all the ways it's not quite right, and I stop. I'm really good at knowing what I don't want. I don't know how to want something enough to stick with it when it gets hard."

She also said: "I'm not angry at my parents. They were trying to give me what they didn't have. But sometimes I wonder—if they'd made me stay in swimming, would I have learned to push through when things got hard? If they'd told me to take chemistry, would I have more options now? I don't know. Maybe I would have just resented them. But at least I would have had something to rebel against. Instead I had nothing but my own choices, and I didn't know how to make them."

REFLECTION QUESTIONS FOR PARENTS

EXPANSION PRINCIPLE

- Emma at thirty-five lacks durable agency—she cannot support herself, has no career trajectory, and depends on us financially. When we let her quit swimming at fourteen, supported her choice to avoid AP Chemistry, told her to "take time to figure things out" after graduation—what were we trying to build? How were we increasing her durable agency for faithful service to God? If not durable agency, what did we think we were forming her toward?

- If Emma told us she was genuinely happy with her life—content with her job, her living situation, her lack of trajectory—would that change our assessment? Does a child's contentment absolve the parent from building durable agency?

- The framework claims that structure builds capacity in ways that freedom alone does not. What assumptions about child development were we operating on, and where did those assumptions come from?

GIFT-LOVE CONSTRAINT

- We believed that deferring to Emma's preferences was the loving choice. But gift-love means seeking the child's genuine good, which sometimes requires doing what the child resists. When Emma wanted to quit swimming, we told ourselves we were respecting her autonomy. Were we? Or were we avoiding the conflict that insisting would have required? What felt harder in that moment—making her continue, or absorbing her unhappiness if we did?

- We both carry wounds from our own upbringings—Michael's father demanded medicine, Jennifer's mother mapped out her entire career. We decided Emma would have what we lacked. But formation is about Emma's needs, not our healing. How much of our parenting philosophy was genuinely calibrated to Emma and not a reaction to our own upbringing?

- Need-love can hide beneath permissiveness just as it hides beneath control. Some parents need compliance;

others need approval. When Emma was happy with our decisions, when she thanked us for "understanding" her, when she told friends how supportive we were—what did that feel like? Did we need to be the parents who never imposed? What would it have cost us, emotionally, to be the parents who required hard things?

ACCOUNTABILITY CONSTRAINT

- The Accountability Constraint addresses adjusting when formation causes breakdown. But Emma never broke down—she drifted. At twenty-two, twenty-six, thirty-two she was home, searching, making no visible progress. We told ourselves she was "finding herself." At what point did explanation become excuse? What signs did we minimize or explain away because confronting them would have required us to question our entire approach?

- The framework emphasizes seeking outside perspective—from church, from professionals, from people who might see what we cannot. During Emma's twenties, did we seek counsel from people who might have challenged our approach? Or did we seek validation from people who shared our philosophy? If someone had told us at twenty-four that Emma was drifting and we needed to change course, how would we have responded?

- Drift is harder to see than breakdown because it accumulates slowly. There is no crisis, no dramatic failure—just years passing without capacity being built. What markers could we have used to recognize drift earlier? If we had set milestones—financial independence by twenty-five, career trajectory by thirty—would we have acted differently? Why didn't we set them?

JURISDICTION CONSTRAINT

- Emma is thirty-five and unmarried. Under the framework, parental directive authority would normally end at marriage—but Emma has never married. This creates ambiguity: does prolonged singleness extend parental jurisdiction indefinitely, or should authority end regardless?

- If we assume that jurisdiction has passed—we cannot now direct her toward nursing or accounting. But we still provide substantial support: housing, insurance, car, loan payments. That support enables her to continue searching without facing the consequences of her choices. Is our continued provision an act of love, or is it preventing the very pressure that might finally produce change? What would happen if we set conditions—or withdrew support entirely?

- We cannot redo Emma's formation. But we can learn from it. If we were raising a fourteen-year-old today, what would we do differently? What specifically would we require that we did not require of Emma? What beliefs about parenting have we abandoned, and what have we come to believe instead?

REFLECTION QUESTIONS FOR CHILD

EXAMINING SELF

- My parents gave me freedom to choose, and I made choices—to quit swimming, to avoid hard courses, to leave programs when they felt wrong. At the time, each choice felt like wisdom. Looking back, what pattern do I see? Was I learning what didn't fit, or was I learning to leave whenever things became difficult? How would I tell the difference?

- If I had a daughter, would I raise her the way my parents raised me? If she wanted to quit something difficult at fourteen, would I let her? If she wanted to avoid demanding courses at sixteen, would I support her? If she came home at twenty-two with no job prospects, would I tell her to take time to figure things out? What does my answer reveal about what I wish my parents had done differently—and what does it demand of me now?

- I am thirty-five. Whatever my parents did or failed to do, the choices now are mine. I can continue to analyze why each path isn't quite right, or I can commit to building something despite imperfection. The framework suggests that meaning often follows competence—that people come to love what they become good at. Am I willing to test that claim? What would it require of me to stay with something long enough to become genuinely competent, even if I don't feel passion for it at the start?

UNDERSTANDING PARENTS

- My parents were reacting against their own upbringings—against fathers who demanded and mothers who controlled. They gave me the freedom they wished they had. But their freedom was shaped by the discipline they resented. They had structure first, then freedom. I had freedom without the structure that makes freedom productive. What did they have at thirty-five that I do not have? What built it in them?

QUESTIONS FOR BOTH

- The current living arrangement communicates something. Emma living at home rent-free, with expenses covered, while working part-time and "figuring things out"—what does that arrangement say about expectations? About consequences? About adulthood? If the arrangement needs to change, what should it become? What timeline? What happens if the new expectations aren't met?

- What would it look like for Emma to build durable agency starting now? Not another exploration, not another certificate that leads nowhere, but sustained commitment to a path that builds real capacity—even if that path isn't perfect, even if Emma doesn't feel passion for it at the start. What specific steps would demonstrate genuine change rather than another pivot? How long would Emma need to persist before anyone could trust that this time is different?

- Ten years from now, Emma will be forty-five. Her parents will be in their seventies. What does Emma need to have built by then—not for her parents' sake, but for her own? What would financial independence, career stability, and genuine adulthood look like for her? What is she willing to sacrifice to get there? What are her parents willing to require—and willing to stop providing—to make that future possible?

CASE STUDY #3

SUCCESS BUT DESTROYED RELATIONSHIP

If formation builds agency but destroys the parent-child relationship, has it succeeded or failed? Is relational outcome part of measuring formation success? Can parents claim gift-love motivation while remaining indifferent to the relational cost of their direction?

Claire is forty-two years old, a successful cardiologist at a major academic medical center. By every objective measure of durable agency, she has succeeded: $300k annual income, full professor, financially independent, married with two children, owns home, provides for aging parents, publishes research, mentors students. She weathered the 2008 recession without crisis, pivoted from private practice to academic medicine when interests shifted, and has resources to invest heavily in her own children's formation.

Her father, Richard, directed her toward medicine from age fourteen. He is also a physician (now retired internist). He made it clear: Claire would attend medical school. Not "Claire could consider medicine" or "let's see if medicine interests you," but "you will be a doctor." He structured her entire high school around this goal: Science Olympiad, hospital volunteering, shadowing experiences, AP sciences prioritized over arts or humanities electives she preferred.

Claire resisted. She wanted to study literature. She loved reading, writing, discussing ideas. Her English teachers told her she had genuine talent. But her father dismissed this: "Writers can't support families. Medicine provides security. You'll thank me later."

Through college and medical school, Claire complied but resented. She found the sciences manageable but joyless. She excelled academically—graduated medical school in top 10%—but felt she was living someone else's life. Her father attended every milestone: white coat ceremony, graduation, residency match. He was visibly proud. Claire felt hollow.

THE RELATIONSHIP DETERIORATION

She completed her cardiology fellowship and built a successful career. By thirty-five, she had the durable agency her father predicted. But the relationship with her father had progressively deteriorated. They spoke rarely and stiffly. When together at family events, conversations were superficial. Richard would point to her success: "See? I was right. Look at what you've achieved."

Claire's response, in therapy at age forty: "He was right about the outcome and wrong about everything else. I have financial security and professional respect. I also have deep resentment toward the person who gave me life. Every time I see him, I remember that my preferences, my voice, my interests meant nothing. He built my career and destroyed our relationship."

At forty-two, Claire speaks to her father a few times per year, mostly about logistics (holidays, grandchildren). She provides financially for him but feels no warmth. She has explicitly told her therapist she will feel "relief, not grief" when he dies. Her father is baffled by her distance: "I gave her everything. I sacrificed for her education. Why is she so cold?"

RICHARD'S PERSPECTIVE

Richard genuinely believes he acted out of love. He didn't seek status through Claire (he already had a successful medical career). He wasn't living vicariously (he already achieved what he directed her toward). He made a calculated judgment that medicine would build durable agency better than literature would. He provided financial support throughout her education without strings. His prediction about durable agency was correct—Claire does have security at forty-two.

Richard sees his daughter's distance as ingratitude. He thinks: "I did everything right. I sacrificed for her future. She has a beautiful life because of my direction. Why can't she see that?"

CLAIRE'S PERSPECTIVE

Claire sees it differently. Her father completely dismissed her expressed preferences and demonstrated talent in literature. He gave no consideration to whether she could build sufficient (if not maximum) agency through writing plus a practical minor. His rigid insistence ("you will be a doctor") left no room for her input. He showed inability to recognize or validate her emotional experience of the formation process. His bafflement at her distance suggests he valued outcome over relationship.

Claire tells her therapist: "My father treated me like an investment portfolio, not a person. He optimized for returns and got them. But portfolios don't have feelings. Portfolios don't resent being managed. I do."

REFLECTION QUESTIONS FOR PARENTS

EXPANSION PRINCIPLE

- Claire has durable agency—but she built it through compliance, not conviction. She never owned the path; she survived it. Does agency count the same when the person carrying it resents how it was built? If Claire had pursued literature and achieved less economic capacity but owned her choices fully, which outcome better serves faithful service to God?

- Durable agency has multiple modes, four of which are: economic self-sufficiency, practical wisdom, trained virtue, and relational capacity. Does this path build all four, or does it overdevelop some while neglecting others? Should one be prioritized or should they all be built equally?

GIFT-LOVE CONSTRAINT

- The framework claims that gift-love becomes sustainable only when a parent's identity is secured in Christ—not in their child's outcomes. When Claire rejected our direction, when she resented us, when she pulled away—what happened to our sense of worth? Were we able to absorb her anger without defensiveness, or did her rejection feel like verdict on us as parents? Where was our identity actually resting?

- Richard showed up at every milestone and paid for Claire's entire education. Claire says he treated her like an investment portfolio. Both things are true. How does a parent give sacrificially—time, money, presence—while also communicating that the child's interior experience matters? What would it have looked like for Richard to direct firmly toward medicine while still making Claire feel heard?

ACCOUNTABILITY CONSTRAINT

- Our child is not falling apart visibly—grades are fine, milestones are being hit. But they are pulling away from us emotionally. What are signs of systemic breakdown that we should look out for?

- We want to build our child's durable agency. But what if our direction builds career success while destroying our relationship with them? How does this impact our grandkids? Should the Accountability Constraint apply to the impact our decisions make on future grandchildren?

- A child can comply without submitting—doing what's required while internally withdrawing. This often looks like success: grades stay high, milestones get met. But the relationship erodes beneath the surface. How would we tell the difference between a child who is genuinely submitting (even through disagreement) and one who is merely complying to survive? What signs would we look for? Does our child feel safe enough to tell us which one they're doing?

JURISDICTION CONSTRAINT

- Richard's direction remained unchanged from the time Claire was fourteen through her completion of medical school. Should Richard's directive authority have begun giving way to advisory influence at some point—and if so, when? At what point did continued insistence drift from formation into control?

REFLECTION QUESTIONS FOR CHILD

EXAMINING SELF

- My father has never apologized because he does not think he did anything wrong. What would reconciliation look like if an apology never comes? What am I waiting for—and what does that waiting cost me?

- My father is aging. Time is running out. If he dies while we are still distant, what will I wish I had done differently? What is stopping me from doing that now?

- My children barely know their grandfather because I keep my distance. What am I teaching them about forgiveness, about family, about how to handle people who have hurt us? What kind of relationship with him might they want—and what right do I have to decide for them?

- My father pushed me toward medicine. I did not choose it, but it gave me real security. What does my resentment tell me about what I expected from him, from the path, from myself? What would it take for the resentment to loosen its grip?

- The framework's discernment process asks the child to seek assessment before reaching a conclusion—to distinguish genuine harm from subjective distress. I never did that. I went silent, built resentment, and reached my verdict alone. What might I have learned if I had sought outside counsel at the time? And would it have changed anything—for the path, for the relationship, or for the story I have told myself since?

UNDERSTANDING PARENTS

- My father genuinely believed that medicine would serve me well. He was not living through me—he already had his own medical career. He paid for my education. He showed up at every milestone. These are not the actions of someone who did not love me. What does it look like to hold "he loved me" and "he hurt me" as both true?

- My father does not understand why I am distant. He truly seems confused about what he did wrong. What about his background and upbringing is contributing to this confusion? What would it require of me to extend grace for what he cannot see—without pretending that the hurt didn't happen?

SUBMISSION AND TRUST

- During medical school, I never told my father what the path was costing me. I stayed silent, performed compliance, and let resentment build where honesty should have been. The framework says that genuine submission stays engaged—voicing disagreement while still moving forward under authority. What stopped me from telling him the truth about my struggle? What might have been different if I had fought to stay connected instead of disappearing into silence?

- I saw my father's direction as control, not love—and I've held that verdict for decades. But the scenario shows a father who already had his own medical career, who paid for my education, who showed up at every milestone. The framework distinguishes covenantal trust from contractual thinking: covenantal trust believes the parent is *for* you even when their judgment seems wrong. How do I reconcile what he did with the story I've told myself about why he did it? What would it require of me to believe he meant my good—even if his methods caused real harm?

QUESTIONS FOR BOTH

- Richard believes he was right. Claire believes she was harmed. Both have evidence. Is it possible that Richard's direction was the correct formation decision *and* that his methods caused real damage—and if so, what does repairing the relationship look like when both parties are right about different things?

- Claire has children who are watching how she relates to her father. What are they learning about conflict, forgiveness, and family? What example is being set—and is it the one she wants to pass down?

CASE STUDY #4

AGENCY WITHOUT FAITH

Can formation succeed by building durable agency while failing at the ultimate purpose of "knowing and faithfully serving God"? If durable agency is instrumental to faithful service, what happens when agency-building destroys the faith that would direct it?

David is thirty-eight, a partner at a major consulting firm earning $350k+ annually. He has extraordinary durable agency: supports his household without strain, extensive savings and investments, provided a down payment for his sister's house, funds his parents' retirement, and sends his children to elite private schools. Professionally respected, intellectually engaged, economically secure.

He also hasn't attended church in fifteen years, considers Christianity "the mythology I grew up with," and describes faith as "psychologically useful for some people but not intellectually serious." His children are being raised secular. His Christian parents are heartbroken.

PARENTS' FORMATION APPROACH

David's parents are devout Christians who immigrated to the U.S. when David was three. They worked manual labor jobs (father as factory worker, mother as seamstress) and sacrificed extensively for David's education. From elementary school forward, they directed every decision toward academic excellence: strict homework schedules, restricted social activities, mandatory tutoring, summers spent in academic programs rather than recreation.

They had a clear rationale: educational achievement was the path to stability in America. They'd experienced the hardship of limited education and wanted David to have security they never had. The direction was motivated by genuine love and concern for his future.

WHAT GOT CROWDED OUT

Alongside the academic focus came systematic neglect of spiritual formation. Church attendance was sporadic because it conflicted with study time. Youth group was forbidden because it took time away from homework. Service projects were replaced with SAT prep. Family prayer became rare because David's schedule was too demanding. Religious education was minimal because academic courses took priority.

The implicit message David internalized: academic achievement is what matters most. Church is something we're culturally attached to but not serious about. God is acknowledged but not prioritized. Success is measured in grades, then income, then status.

THE DRIFT

Through high school and college, David's faith became progressively more nominal. He attended an elite university, encountered intellectual critiques of Christianity, found Christian community uninteresting compared to career-focused peers, and drifted away. His parents noticed but didn't intervene forcefully—they were proud of his academic success and hoped faith would "come back later."

By his mid-twenties, David was functionally secular. By thirty, explicitly so. He now views Christianity as cultural heritage rather than truth. His parents pray for him and grieve deeply. They also recognize their own contribution: "We pushed so hard for his education that we lost his soul."

THE CURRENT SITUATION

David doesn't see his secularism as a loss. From his perspective, he succeeded. He escaped the economic limitations his parents experienced. He provided for them in their old age. He's living the American dream they wanted for him. That it cost his faith is, to him, just maturation—moving past childhood mythology into adult rationality.

His children are being raised without religious formation of any kind. David's parents see this as generational spiritual death: they raised a son who has economic capacity to bless his children but instead raises them without God.

REFLECTION QUESTIONS FOR PARENTS

EXPANSION PRINCIPLE

- The framework says that durable agency serves "faithful service to God." David has extraordinary capacity—money, skills, influence—but no faith to direct it. In what ways did our parenting treat economic capacity as the goal rather than a means?

- If the purpose is missing, has durable agency actually been built? What would formation look like that kept the purpose and the capacity together?

- Durable agency has multiple modes, four of which are economic self-sufficiency, practical wisdom, trained virtue, and relational capacity. David has extraordinary economic capacity. But what about the others?

GIFT-LOVE CONSTRAINT

- We genuinely wanted David to have the security we never had. When studying and church conflicted, we chose studying. Was that choice driven by gift-love—genuine concern for David's long-term good—or by our own anxiety about economic stability? How do we tell the difference between directing a child toward security for their sake versus for our own peace of mind?

- When David succeeded, we felt pride. When he drifted from faith, we felt grief—but we did not intervene. What does it reveal about our motives that academic failure would have prompted immediate action, but spiritual failure did not?

ACCOUNTABILITY CONSTRAINT

- David did not reject faith because he was never exposed to it—he rejected it because what he experienced felt shallow compared to the intellectual rigor he encountered elsewhere. The Accountability Constraint watches for breakdown, but spiritual drift happens quietly inside. What would it have looked like to form David's faith with the same rigor and intentionality we gave his academics—not just requiring attendance, but engaging the hardest questions before he left for college?

- During David's formation, what voices did we seek out—and what voices did we avoid? When we chose studying over church, who in our lives had standing to question that priority? The framework says that parents need diverse outside perspective, including voices they expect to disagree with. Looking back, who might have challenged our approach if we had invited them to? What kept us from seeking—or hearing—that perspective?

JURISDICTION CONSTRAINT

- We used our authority to direct David's academics because we could see the results—grades, test scores, admissions. Spiritual formation has no equivalent metrics. How does a parent direct with intentionality toward something they cannot measure? What would it have looked like to exercise the same authority over David's spiritual development when we had no GPA to track, no milestone to hit, and no way to know if it was working?

- Our authority has ended. David is thirty-eight. He has made his choices—choices that break our hearts. What does honoring him as an adult look like when we believe those choices are leading him away from God? How do we stay close without every conversation becoming an attempt to change his mind?

REFLECTION QUESTIONS FOR CHILD

EXAMINING SELF

- I rejected my parents' faith. What version of Christianity did I actually encounter—and what versions have I never seriously explored? When I found arguments against faith convincing, what made them persuasive? What would it look like to engage the strongest versions of Christianity rather than the version I grew up with?

- My parents grieve my choices. I find their grief frustrating. But they are aging, and time is limited. What kind of relationship do I want with them for whatever years remain?

UNDERSTANDING PARENTS

- My parents sacrificed enormously for me. They worked exhausting jobs so I could have opportunities they never had. They do not want my money—they want me to share their faith. What does it look like to honor them?

- My parents' faith shaped how they raised me—including the pressure that drove me away. What parts of their faith did I reject because of how they practiced it, rather than what it actually teaches? What would it look like to evaluate Christianity on its own terms rather than through the lens of their mistakes?

QUESTIONS FOR BOTH

- Can we have a genuine relationship across this divide? What does mutual respect look like when we disagree about the deepest things—about whether God exists, about what happens after death, about what life is for?

- David's children are being raised without faith. What role, if any, can grandparents play in their grandchildren's spiritual formation when the parents have rejected that faith? Where is the line between sharing what they believe and undermining David's authority as a parent?

- Ten years from now, what would each of you need to see to believe this relationship was handled well? Not agreement—that may never come. But something better than distance, silence, or grief that never gets spoken.

- David has built extraordinary economic capacity but no faith to direct it. His parents built deep faith but limited economic capacity. Each generation had something the other lacked. What are lessons learned that could be applied to the next generation?

CASE STUDY #5

MISSIONS VS. DURABLE AGENCY

Does the framework permit—or even require—parents to forbid paths that serve kingdom purposes but foreclose traditional durable agency? What happens when the child wants to maximize faithful service while minimizing economic capacity?

Ethan is eighteen, a high school senior with exceptional academic credentials: 3.9 GPA, 1520 SAT, National Merit Scholar. He has acceptance letters from three good universities, including his state flagship with a full scholarship. His parents are middle-class Evangelical Christians—father is an accountant, mother is an elementary school teacher. They have saved diligently for Ethan's education and see law as an ideal path: high durable agency, the ability to advocate for others, and a respectable profession.

Ethan wants to decline the scholarship and attend a small Bible college to prepare for overseas missions. Specifically, he wants to become a long-term missionary to unreached groups in Southeast Asia. He's been on three short-term mission trips, learned some Mandarin, connected with a missionary organization that works in restricted-access countries, and feels deeply called to this work.

ETHAN'S VISION

Ethan's plan: Four years at Bible college studying theology, biblical languages, and cross-cultural ministry. Then join a missionary organization that places workers in Southeast Asia under business or teaching visas (since direct missionary work is illegal in many target countries). Live on $25k–$30k annual support from churches and donors. Spend 20–30 years serving the underground church, translating Scripture, and discipling believers in a region where Christianity is severely restricted.

Ethan argues: "Jesus called disciples to leave everything and follow Him. Paul was a tentmaker, but his real work was gospel ministry. If I spend my twenties building a career, I'll get comfortable, accumulate responsibilities, and never go. God is calling me now, to this work, and you're asking me to choose financial security over obedience to Him."

PARENTS' CONCERNS

Ethan's parents see this path as economically catastrophic: Bible college costs $20k/year with no scholarship (they'd pay $80k total versus $0 for state school). A Bible college degree has minimal economic value if missions doesn't work out. If Ethan marries and has children, he'd raise them in poverty abroad or struggle financially if he returns to the U.S. At forty, missionary-Ethan would have no retirement savings, no home equity, no transferable professional skills, and no capacity to support aging parents or invest in his own children's formation.

They propose an alternative: attend state school on scholarship, then law school, build a career foundation for 5–7 years—then either pursue missions from a position of financial stability or support missions financially, giving more over a lifetime than

Ethan would ever earn on the field. This way, Ethan could serve kingdom purposes while building durable agency that provides options if circumstances change.

OUTSIDE COUNSEL

Ethan's youth pastor and missionary mentor both support his vision. The youth pastor says: "We need young people willing to sacrifice comfort for kingdom advancement. Ethan has a rare calling. Don't quench the Spirit." The missionary mentor says: "I went to the field at twenty-two. If I'd built a career first, I never would have gone. The harvest is urgent. Financial security can wait."

Ethan's parents have also sought counsel. Their pastor is cautious: "Many young people feel called to missions after emotional experiences on short-term trips. Some genuinely are called. Others are responding to the moment. How do you distinguish?" An older missionary couple (now in their sixties, recently returned from the field) share a sobering perspective: "We went at twenty-three, served thirty-five years, loved the work, no regrets about calling. But we also watched many missionaries burn out, leave the field for health or family reasons, and return to the U.S. in their forties with no savings, no job prospects, and children who struggled. Not everyone who feels called at eighteen sustains that calling through the difficulties of the field. Having options matters."

THE DECISION POINT

Ethan's parents must decide whether to pay for Bible college (implicitly endorsing the missions path) or insist he attend state school with the scholarship (potentially opposing a genuine calling). They have authority to refuse to pay for Bible college. But should they use it?

REFLECTION QUESTIONS FOR PARENTS

EXPANSION PRINCIPLE

- If Ethan serves faithfully for thirty years but returns at fifty with no savings, no career, and limited ability to provide for aging parents or invest in his own children's formation—was the formation successful? Does faithfulness to God require the capacity to fulfill other obligations, or can it bypass them?

- The framework says formation should prepare children for faithful service to God. What does that look like for household formation? Have we talked honestly with him about it?

- Ethan's children would be raised on missionary support in a foreign culture. What impact would this have on our future grandkids and how much should this be taken into consideration?

GIFT-LOVE CONSTRAINT

- Would we feel differently if Ethan wanted to pursue domestic ministry—seminary, pastoral work, a church staff position? If overseas missions bothers us more than local ministry, what is driving that difference? Is it the ministry itself, or the geography and the uncertainty?

- We are funding a state school but not Bible college. When we made that decision, were we directing Ethan toward durable agency for faithful service to God—or away from a path that frightens us? What's the difference, and how would we know?

ACCOUNTABILITY CONSTRAINT

- What would systemic breakdown look like if Ethan pursues missions? What would it look like if he pursues engineering under our direction? Are we more equipped to recognize one kind of breakdown than the other—and does that bias our decision?

- If Ethan is on a mission field in a restricted-access country, how would we know if he's breaking down? Who would tell us? What accountability structures would need to exist for the Accountability Constraint to function at all?

- If Ethan burns out on the mission field and returns at thirty-five, what will that failure reveal? The framework argues breakdown shows only what didn't work—not that he was "called" to something else.

JURISDICTION CONSTRAINT

- We have the authority to refuse funding for Bible college. But having authority and knowing when to use it are different questions. Ethan is eighteen—legally an adult, but still being formed. How does his age affect how we exercise our authority?

- Ten years from now, Ethan is twenty-eight—independent, outside our authority. If he's struggling on the mission field and calls asking for help, what do we say? What do we do? If we blocked Bible college and he's now stable but distant, telling us he's never forgiven us for killing his calling—what do we say? What do we do? How we imagine these conversations reveals what we're trying to protect now?

REFLECTION QUESTIONS FOR CHILD

EXAMINING SELF

- I believe God is calling me to missions. But the framework says calling cannot be known beforehand. How do I hold my strong desire to serve with the possibility that I'm mistaking preference for divine direction? How do I weigh this against the authority God has given my parents?

- I want to go now—not later. Where does that urgency come from? Is it a conviction that will sustain through decades of difficulty, or an excitement that might fade when the path gets hard?

UNDERSTANDING PARENTS

- My parents are not opposing God—they are trying to steward my formation. They have watched missionaries burn out, seen families struggle on support, and know what it takes to sustain a household over decades. What might they see about the cost of this path that I cannot yet see from where I stand?

SUBMISSION AND TRUST

- If I go to a state school, I can comply or I can submit. Compliance does what's required while withdrawing internally—going through the motions while building resentment in silence. Submission stays engaged through disagreement—voicing my perspective, hearing my parents' reasoning, and moving forward without bitterness even when I still disagree. Which am I capable of? What would genuine submission look like if I walk this path?

QUESTIONS FOR BOTH

- The parents' alternative—state school, then law, then missions later—sounds reasonable. But the missionary mentor says "if I'd built a career first, I never would have gone." Is that a warning or an excuse? Does delayed obedience to a genuine calling become disobedience—or does it become wisdom? How would we know the difference?

- Ethan's youth pastor supports missions. His parents' pastor urges caution. The older missionary couple says both are true—the calling may be real and the cost may be higher than Ethan imagines. When godly counsel conflicts, how do we decide who to listen to? What makes one voice more credible than another on a question like this?

- What would it look like to make this decision in a way that preserves our relationship no matter the outcome? Can we disagree and still stay close—or is this becoming a fight someone has to win?

- Ten years from now, Ethan will be twenty-eight. What outcome would we all look back on with gratitude—not because everyone got what they wanted, but because we handled this well and stayed a family through it?

Made in the USA
Coppell, TX
11 June 2026

79901341R00104